Zen and the Art of the Monologue

Zen and the Art of the Monologue

Jay Sankey

2

Routledge

New York and London

Published in 2000 by
Routledge
29 West 35th St.
New York, NY 10001

Published in Great Britain by
Routledge
11 New Fetter Lane
London EC4P 4EE

Routledge is an imprint of the Taylor & Francis Group.
Copyright © 2000 by Routledge

Printed in the United States of America on acid-free paper.

10 9 8 7 6 5 4 3 2 1

Library of Congress Cataloging-in-Publication Data

Sankey, Jay, 1963-
    Zen and the art of the monologue / Jay Sankey.
        p. cm.
    Includes bibliographical references.
    ISBN 0-87830-094-5 (pbk.)
    1. Monologue. I. Title.

PN1530 .S26 2000
792--dc21

                                                        00-055339

I have had to strip myself naked. One does not like what one sees then, and one is afraid of what others will see and do. To challenge one's deepest, most nameless fears is also to challenge the heavens. It is to drag yourself and everything and everyone you love to the attention of the fiercest of the gods; who may not forgive your impertinence, who may not spare you.

—James Baldwin

Oddly, the more personal something is, the more universal it is as well. When we dig deeper to truthful experiences, that's the work that really touches people and connects us all.

—Bill Watterson,
creator of the cartoon strip
Calvin and Hobbes

The practice of zen is forgetting the self in the act of uniting with something else.

—Koun Yamada

This book is dedicated to my very dear friends
Jason Maloney, David Peck, and David Acer
for always making me feel that my thoughts
and feelings are worth sharing.
And to Meredith. Sweet angel, it was worth the wait.

Contents

Foreword

To believe that what is true for you is true for all men. That is genius.
—Henry Miller

Standing while others are seated can be a brazen act. But to stand there in front of everyone and boldly share your thoughts and feelings can be the act of a revolutionary, a social dissident—or at least an upstart. For such an act reflects a belief that is still a tad heretical, even in these modern times: the belief in taking one's own personal experience seriously; the belief that, as personal as it is, it is nonetheless a part of a larger, collective truth.

This belief presents a great many challenges, both to yourself and to others. After all, what are you to them? And why should they spend even a single moment listening to you talk? Taking one's own inner life seriously and having a fervent desire to share it with others also dares the ego to take the wheel, drive to the closest greasy spoon, tuck a napkin into its shirt collar, and shovel as much crap into itself as possible, bloating it up to a truly monstrous size.

Yet for me, so much of standing up and speaking my mind in front of strangers comes down to trust—trust in the act of sharing; trust in myself, that I can handle being misunderstood, and even more frightening, being *understood;* and most of all, trust that perhaps none of us are really strangers after all.

At first glance, this may seem to be a book of questions and answers about monologuing. But in truth it is a small book about an enormous subject: unique perspective and the art and craft of sharing. For example, while the questions reflect a wide range of perspectives, the answers reflect but one. Mine. Actually, my own background in the art of monologuing lies much more in the area of solo shows than that of soliloquies and short monologues performed for acting auditions or within the context of a larger play. This book does, however, explore a great many aspects of the monologue form, including the use of monologues for acting auditions and the role of monologues in full plays.

Our experiences give rise to our answers, whether in matters artistic or metaphysic. And though my own answers in the realm of the monologue are based on experience (lending the book some credibility), I believe perhaps an even more valid answer to any of the questions asked in this book is, It's really up to you. Or, Experience and find out for yourself.

Why then did I bother writing this book? Well, I remember once reading about how, around the turn of this century, professional safecrackers would routinely brush sandpaper across their fingertips to make them all the more sensitive to the task at hand. Think of this book then as a couple hundred sheets of sandpaper, written in the hope that as you flip through them, you too will become a little more sensitive and receptive to the fascinating personal challenges involved in the writing and performing of your own monologue. Your story—and ours.

Jay Sankey
Toronto, Canada
August 2000

1

The Monologue

What is a monologue?

Words have the power to destroy or heal. When words are both true and kind, they can change our world.
—Shunryu Suzuki

A monologue is a predominantly verbal presentation given by a single person featuring a collection of ideas, often loosely assembled around one or more themes. Note that I do not define it as a *strictly* verbal presentation; many, though certainly not all, successful monologuists also employ nonverbal elements to great effect, such as, their use of facial expressions and hand gestures, along with a variety of props and stage devices.

Is it okay to have a friend perform my monologue with me?

No, it's not okay. In fact, it's very wrong. It's a *monologue,* coming from the Greek word *mono,* which means "singular," "one," "alone." Just you. No friends. No family. No supporting actors. No highly publicized cameos. You are alone onstage: accept it.

How does a monologue differ from a play?

Zen insists on personal experience and insight.

—Irmgard Schloegl

Both a play and a monologue have a script, a performance, and (on a good night) an audience . But while a play usually features several performers, a monologue has but one. A play, with its usual cast of several performers, has much more with which to appeal to not only the audience's eyes but their minds and hearts as well. Several actors make group dynamics possible and provide a much greater variety of physical actions onstage. This in turn gives many more possibilities for an engaging narrative.

As a monologuist, you have none of this. From one moment to the next the audience's attention remains solely yours. But what incredible freedom! This combination of intense attention and personal freedom is in fact one of the most powerful attractions to the monologue form.

Of course, such freedom also represents a very real danger, especially to the vain or inexperienced, as it offers more than enough rope for the impetuous to hang themselves. Monologues also tend to explore a single event or theme from various intellectual and emotional vantage points, rather than, like plays, telling a long and complicated story. In most monologues, not a lot actually "happens." Again, this is probably because action is not one of the natural strengths of the form. Nevertheless, an hour of mere "telling" can get excruciatingly dull for performers and audiences alike, which is why really effective monologues tend to explore and examine the most intimate contents of a human soul. In response to the intensity of an entire audience's silent, respectful, even expectant focus, the monologuist works to share his or her most personal thoughts with equal intensity.

What is the difference between a monologue, a soliloquy, and a speech?

The script is the actor's greatest enemy.

—Sanford Meisner

One of the most obvious differences is their typical *length*. Speeches and soliloquies are often only five, ten, or maybe at most fifteen minutes long, while monologues are commonly forty, sixty, even ninety minutes in length. This is precisely why they are sometimes referred to as "one-person shows."

Ronald Of Nazareth

But even more significantly, when someone gives a speech, there is not only a definite "prewritten" feel to it, but also often a sense that the speaker (who is seldom truly "performing") believes he or she *knows something.* Speeches are usually more about ideas than feelings. And while a soliloquy can be an extremely emotional experience for both the performer and the audience, soliloquies too still tend to feel scripted. All too often actors performing soliloquies seem more focused on respecting the carefully worded texts they hold fervently in their minds than on truly communing with the breathing audience seated in front of them.

To my mind, the very spirit of the monologue form is based on the audience's intense involvement, with the goal being a sharing more than a "delivering" or "telling." And it is this emphasis upon profound *sharing* that colors much of my thinking about the craft of the monologue.

On both sides of the footlights, monologues simply have a different feel. With the performer striving to cultivate a powerful sense of intimacy with the audience, the best monologues seem more like a chatty, stream-of-consciousness confessional than a prepared speech or even a moving soliloquy. And by "intimacy" I mean a powerful sense of connection resulting from a heightened awareness of a shared reality. In fact, monologuists typically try to establish a "sitting across the table in a coffee shop" rapport with their audience, so they are not so much "the performer" as an extremely articulate and impassioned confidante on a roll. Consequently, monologuists commonly break from their scripts, going off on a totally unprepared tangent before returning to their carefully written scripts. The form simply has a sublimely unfettered, trusting, and even freewheeling sensibility.

DO SIAMESE TWINS REALLY UNDERSTAND DOUBLE ENTENDRES?

Yes and no. They understand them on an intellectual level, but seldom find them engaging or amusing on an emotional level. After years of intensive studying and research I have concluded (I believe definitively) that this is because the twins, connected at the hip as they are, sense that double entendres subtly echo their own peculiar physical circumstance, and so find them vaguely unsettling. Consequently, if you ever spot one or more Siamese twins in the crowd during a performance, I advise you to stick to puns and knock-knock jokes. Twins, connected or not, love a good knock-knock joke; each of them intuitively feels capable of either relating to or identifying with one of the two "knocks."

What is the difference between a stand-up comedy set and a monologue?

While a stand-up comedy set tends to be primarily cathartic, I believe a monologue typically explores a greater intellectual and emotional range. Monologues are also generally more interested in actual events and powerful feelings, though there are certainly comics who specialize in the telling of true stories. Bill Cosby and Lenny Bruce were masters of this kind of stand-up.

And again, the implicit relationship between the performer and the audience is very different during a comedy show in a club than it is during a monologue in a theater. In a comedy club, the crowd comes to laugh. No less, and very little more. And undoubtedly, the intensity of these two simple desires, to laugh (the audience) and to make them laugh (the performer), makes for a powerful experience. But I am not convinced stand-up comedy has a monologue's potential for a true transformation of both the audience members and the performer.

Audience expectation also profoundly influences the total experience. Did they come to laugh or come to learn? To drink or to explore? To watch or to participate? All of these distinctions account for many of the differences between stand-up comedy and monologuing.

What makes the monologue form so special?

I am not going to show you my art. I am going to share it with you. If I show it to you it becomes an exhibition, and in time it will be pushed so far into the back of your mind that it will be lost. But by sharing it with you, you will not only retain it forever, but I too will improve.
—Ed Parker, karate master

I sometimes think of a monologue as a kind of "talking cure." Not just for the performer, but for the audience too. One person sharing a collection of some of her most intimate musings and speculations within an artfully established and purposefully thematic context can be a fascinating catalyst for all kinds of sharing, between the performer and the audience, and among the audience members themselves, both during and after the performance. Ultimately, a monologue is a means of revelation. Truths are revealed, both familiar and foreign, and in a manner as simple and straightforward as it is courageous. One person stands up in front of a group of strangers, and in the process the souls of all present are unearthed and illuminated. Truly, a wonderful thing.

What is the result of this kind of profound theatrical sharing?

The urge to transcend self-conscious selfhood is a principal appetite of the soul.

—Aldous Huxley

Powerful theatrical experiences yield a transformation of both the audience and the performer, a slight breaking down of at least a few of the subtle distinctions that existed before this sharing. Many of us, especially in Western culture, walk around with tragically fixed ideas of "I am this" and "they are that." Yet humans are much more alike than not and share so much more in common than our egos often would like to admit. Many of our givens about how different we all are only serve to separate and divide us from the truth of our one, shared state.

But through artistic encounters like the monologue, even as we witness the expression of this or that unique perspective, we at the same time experience a profound underlying similarity. A sharedness. And it is this, above all else, that I believe is the most valuable outcome of the performance of any monologue.

Do dyslexics read books from the back to the front?

No, that's just silly. But I often have wondered what it must be like to sometimes see a word backward. To be driving down the road, let's say on your way to a restaurant, and to look up at a stop sign and see the word *pots*. Then at the restaurant to be handed a desserts menu and see the word *stressed*. And even on your way out of the restaurant, when you're paying your bill at the cash register, to look down at the bowl marked TIPS and wonder why they want you to spit on all those coins. And finally, assuming it was an especially spicy meal, to have someone offer you a Tums, only to see the word *smut*. Must be weird. In fact, perhaps out of respect for this unusual visual malady, we should always spell the word *cixelsyd*. Just a thought.

Why should I write and perform a monologue?

The more fully we give our energy, the more it returns to us.
—Master Rinzai

Because it's a challenge, because it's fun—for a million reasons! Monologues offer a variety of writing and performing opportunities unlike any other theatrical form. You and your audience share a wonderful intimacy and an unusual degree of focused attention, resulting in an incomparable opportunity for an exchange of perspectives. You share yours directly through your script and performance, and they share theirs with you indirectly through their response. Seldom do both performers and audience have the opportunity to drink so deeply of each other's vision.

Monologuing is an extremely pliant form, especially given the expectations of many monologue audiences. I certainly wouldn't say their expectations are low, but they are seldom restrictive. Monologue audiences realize that they usually are in store for a performance without a typically linear narrative or cast of characters. They do however expect (hope?) that the performer will nonetheless take them on a fascinating and perhaps even thrilling ride.

Along with these forgiving audience expectations, the form itself encourages the performer to jump freely from one subject or theme to another, and so a monologue is also the ideal way to both explore and showcase your abilities as a performer, writer, art director, musician, and so on. And to think that you can perform a monologue anytime and anywhere! It is without a doubt one of the most direct and intense means of "birthing" your unique creative perspective—the way you and only you experience and see the world. And in sharing this perspective with others, you will in turn gain a sublime confidence in yourself as a performer, as a writer, and perhaps best of all, as a human being with a valid outlook on this thing we call life!

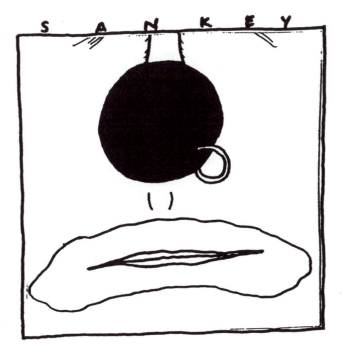

Hip Clown

Is it a good idea to write a small part in my show for my pet dog, cat, or budgie?

It really depends. Can your pet, as cute as it may well be, be trusted to act professionally at all times? Is your pet union or nonunion? Is it good with accents? What about its comedic timing? These are all extremely important questions. And even if after careful consideration you decide to write your pet into the script, I suggest you give your pet very few lines, and even these should not be essential. I remember once watching a Scandinavian woman perform a two-hour monologue with a live, chittering otter tied to her back. It was terrible theater, but I can't say I'll ever forget it.

What exactly is Zen?

When you seek it, you cannot find it.

—Traditional Zen koan

Actually, nothing about Zen is exact. *Zen* is the Japanese word for meditation. Zen is also a school of Buddhism (strongly influenced by Taoism) that was developed in China during the sixth century A.D. The Buddha taught that we are each an integral part of a single, unified reality— that all is one. The Buddha also taught that our ego or "self" tends to delude us into both thinking and feeling that we are somehow separate from the world and other people. This tendency, the Buddha said, is in turn the cause for all of life's sufferings. Many of the cultures of the world are based on a variety of beliefs and practices that actually nurture this sense of separation rather than combat it. But through Zen, we are awakened from this "cultural trance," our self is silenced, and we are returned, if only for a few moments, to our original state of grace.

Sometimes one of the best ways to try to describe something, especially something open to a great many misunderstandings, is to take a few moments to state what it is not. Zen is not a religion. Zen is not ritualistic. And though it is said to have both "masters" and "students," when it comes to Zen there is nothing to teach and nothing to learn. In this way, Zen defies analysis. Its goal is experience, not understanding, the connection between things rather than the things themselves.

What does Zen have to do with monologuing?

Zen is simply a voice crying, "Wake up! Wake up!"
—Maha Sthavira Sangharashita

To my mind, both Zen and monologuing share many of the same goals and even reflect a similar spirit. Both are passionately interested in the cultivation of personal expression and the exploring of a larger, unified reality. Monologuing also presents a wonderful variety of challenges to our fragile hearts and troubled minds, and adopting certain Zen attitudes of acceptance and flexibility will not only help us meet these challenges but actually change our relationship to them, transforming them not just into allies, but into aspects of our own being, a being that, even while onstage delivering lines written a year ago, strives to be "in the moment." Here. Now. This too is Zen.

What sort of background do you bring to the study of monologuing?

I've always been fascinated with communication—with hearing and being heard. Connection. Maybe it's because I'm a middle child (birth order theory suggests that I never got as much attention as my younger sister, "the baby," or my older brother, "the first child"). Then again, maybe it's because I'm not a particularly tall person (5'5") and what I call "communication" is really an essential desire to be in control, in reaction to my inherent sense of smallness. Or maybe it's simply that I have an unusually strong thirst for intimacy (my preferred theory). Who knows? Maybe it's a bit of all three along with a few dozen more.

Whatever the psychological impetus, this passion for communication has thus far taken me on quite a wild ride through a variety of disciplines. As a very young boy I was drawn to music, especially the harp. Then in my early teens I was bitten by the magic bug and spent much of the next ten years performing at parties and ceaselessly practicing sleight-of-hand. Card tricks, coin tricks, really the "theater of the hands." I've also always tended to approach things in a somewhat analytical fashion, and magic was no exception. Not content to focus on the merely technical aspects of illusion, misdirection, and staging, I spent a lot of time thinking about the psychological and emotional implications of performing "tricks" for people. As a result, in my early twenties I began creating my own routines, writing books on the subject, and touring North America and Europe as a lecturer.

After graduating from the University of Toronto with a combined degree in philosophy and psychology, I spent a couple of years as a copywriter at a small advertising agency. I can't say it was the most enjoyable job I've ever had, but having to work with both the written and spoken word for (at least) eight hours a day, five days a week, I learned a great deal about both the craft and discipline of writing and editing.

For the last ten years or so I've also been spending much of my time performing stand-up comedy, thanks to which I've had many opportunities to work in radio and television. This most recent of my careers has taught me alot about self-promotion and performing in front of large groups of people on an almost nightly basis. And of course over the last decade I have also written, performed, and produced a number of monologues, including *Contents under Pressure* (1995) and *Borrowed Breath* (1998). As luck would have it, *Contents* caught the eye of a Canadian production company and was later produced for television, airing on the Bravo! channel as part of their Spoken Arts series.

IS IT REALLY BETTER TO TEACH A MAN TO FISH THAN IT IS TO SIMPLY GIVE HIM A FISH?

Not really. You see, if you give a man a fish and feed him for but a single day, he will necessarily have to come back to you tomorrow looking for more fish. And if you give him another fish then, he will nonetheless need you to feed him the day after that, i.e., Tuesday. And in fact, by establishing this desperate need-oriented cycle, it's a very simple matter to get the poor bastard hooked on heroin, where the *real* money is.

If instead you go to the trouble to teach the guy to fish, he'll inevitably spend much of his time drinking beer, telling lies, and wearing a stupid-looking hat. Never a good idea. So it's either a burgeoning business in the distribution of hard drugs or the creating of yet another alcoholic, untrustworthy, and poorly dressed individual. It's your choice.

What is the difference between a soliloquy and a monologue, or "one-person show"?

A soliloquy, such as Shakespeare's "To be or not to be," usually is performed within the context of a much larger chain of events and against the backdrop of many other characters. It is a small part of a considerably larger enterprise. Within the context of a one-person show there is, strictly speaking, no real "monologue." Rather, the entire script is a single monologue. This essential difference of context and theatrical purpose makes for a variety of distinctions between traditional soliloquies and a one-person show.

Take for example the matter of perspective. When a monologue or soliloquy appears within the context of a play consisting of many actors and a lot of dialogue, the monologue usually offers a particular character an opportunity to share with the audience a heightened instance of his or her perspective on the events of the play. Such monologues are also often a welcome change of pace from the play's long stretches of dialogue.

This is not the case with a one-person show. Certainly the most effective of these shows explore a variety of rhythms and pacings. But the actor cannot rely on the novelty of a single voice, suddenly featured and concentrated, because the *entire script* of a one-person show is just such an isolated expression. Again, it's a matter of context. In a sixty-minute one-person show or solo theater, rhythms are subtly established, varied, and broken, all within the boundaries of a single voice (even if that one actor's voice is expressed through several distinct characters).

This collection of rhythms and pacings in turn profoundly influences the sole actor's physical involvement. As the minutes tick by and the sentences flow into paragraphs and then into pages, such a monologue is not unlike a slowly lengthening string of railway cars, each attached to the other. Over such an extended period of time, the monologue gains a kind of weight, even a theatrical momentum.

This is not so with shorter soliloquies. Within the context of a traditional play, with its many actors and complicated series of events, such brief monologues do not acquire the

Amateur Fire Juggler

same kind of weight or life. Certainly they can be stirring and captivating (and often even the most memorable part of the play), but they still exist to serve the play as a whole. Solo theater serves nothing but itself.

What is the role of a soliloquy in a play?

It really depends upon the particular goals of the playwright. However, traditionally a soliloquy holds the key to that character's perspective of the play's events or overall themes. In this way, just as it has been said that "behind all great art there is great science," such speeches are an instance of effective craft in that they offer a character the perfect vehicle through which he can share his thoughts and feelings with the audience.

What is the difference between delivering a soliloquy as part of a play and delivering a speech as an entire one-person show?

As an actor onstage, ask yourself this: Who am I talking to? As simple as this question may seem, it is actually one of the more important and profound questions in all of theater. Whether or not there are other actors onstage, when delivering a speech you must still consider whether your character is speaking to the audience or merely "talking out loud." Then again, maybe you are talking to God or even talking to yourself—while at the same time being fully aware of the fact that another character in the play is eavesdropping. These are the very considerations that will profoundly influence the style and spirit of your delivery.

Is a speech the ultimate test of an actor's abilities?

Not necessarily. Given that a speech is an instance of concentrated acting, it is understandable that people commonly think of speeches as the true test of an actor's gifts. But while some actors are strong monologuists, they are less effective dialoguists. They simply are not as adept at nurturing a chemistry between themselves and their fellow actors. Then again, some less inspired monologuists are exceptional performers when it comes to sharing a stage with other members of the cast.

As usual, it really comes down to the actor's natural abilities, the kind of acting she most enjoys and her own personal growth goals. Some performers stick very closely to their strengths, while others are forever challenging themselves in hopes of becoming more skilled, well-rounded practitioners.

How can I best prepare to perform a speech?

Many acting teachers suggest that one can only do justice to a speech to the degree to which one understands the particular speech's role in (and relationship to) the entire play. What has happened to the character up to that point? And how does the speech further the goals and themes of the play as a whole? You will notice that a great many published collections of speeches (soliloquys, really, or else long speeches to another character—one-half of a dialogue) offer brief summaries of the play's actions up to the point of the speech along with a short sketch of the character.

This makes a great deal of sense, but I think it is equally important to ask yourself, Why am I going to use this particular speech in this or that audition? Answer: To showcase your abilities as an actor and to capture the attention of the producer, director, or casting agent! Certainly you can choose to deliver a certain speech within well-established theatrical and interpretive guidelines, but there are other ways, too. Instead, you may want to consider exploring a classic speech in a less traditional fashion. Not only might you grow in ways you cannot imagine, but you may even create a uniquely engaging version of that same classic.

I am reminded of the expression "new wine in old bottles," which you might think of as a distinction between form and content, or "what you do" and "how you do it." In the arts, many individuals have had great success by doing something traditional in a nontraditional manner. Certain film versions of Shakespeare's plays fall into this category. People also often have success doing something nontraditional, but in a traditional manner. Imagine a painting of a computer, but done with brush techniques that mimic the painting style of a Renoir or even a Cézanne.

However, given the logical permutations of this "wine and bottles" analogy, there are two other possible approaches apart from putting new wine in old bottles and old wine in new bottles. You could choose to deliver a brand-new speech in a brand-new way, or an old speech in an old way. Note that these two approaches are typically less effective than the first two, and for very good reason. Doing something new in a new way is often just too...new. There is nothing for an audience to hold onto, no common point of reference. And as for doing something old in an old way—well, it's just plain dull and predictable. Both can be fatal for a creative project.

As for preparing to perform a speech, my advice is *don't* read the suggested character outline or even the description of the events leading up to the beginning of the speech in the overall play. You can always read those later. But you can't *unread* them. So why limit your own creativity and intuitions from the very beginning when you don't have to?

Why not at least start by flipping through a collection of speeches, avert your gaze from the editor's outlines and character descriptions, and focus strictly on the speeches themselves? Read a few aloud and let your imagination wander. Invent the character and theatrical context. Take the time to experiment with one or two that strike your fancy. And then, only after having developed a definite and unique creative relationship with this or that speech, do I suggest you read those very interpretive words of the editor.

Of course, out of respect for the playwright it is always a good idea to have a strong grasp of a particular speech's role in the overall play. But again, there are a great many resources to refer to when it comes to such matters. There are far fewer resources in place to encourage and protect your own unique perspective and imagination! That's pretty much up to you. Remember, the editor may well know the play, but only you know your strengths as an actor.

How should I choose a speech to perform?

I try never to lose sight of the simple fact that a speech, like a song or a magic trick or even an advertisement for a chocolate bar, is an instance of both expression and communication. Yes, you are expressing yourself through the speech, but if you want anyone to listen to you, even for a moment, keep in mind that what happens next may depend as much on what is going on in your audience's minds as in your own.

All right, so you are trying to choose a speech to perform. Whether you plan to deliver it to your family over dessert, to your fellow students in acting class, or to a director at an audition, I think there is a lot to be said for avoiding a speech your potential audience already knows well. Certainly, if you have an especially inspired approach to a hackneyed speech, or (better yet) you have developed a character and an attitude that actually takes into account and implicitly comments upon the speech's cliché status, that could be very effective indeed. But barring such ingenious tactics, why not choose a speech that your audience hasn't heard a million times before?

Another factor you definitely should take into account is your particular strengths as an actor. What is the general mood of the speech? Morose? Blissful? Jealous? It is not uncommon for an actor to feel at least a little more drawn to one hue of the emotional rainbow than to another. Being aware of these emotional tendencies in yourself can serve you extremely well when it comes to choosing an especially appropriate speech.

Ideally, you are looking for a speech that both inspires and challenges you, one which literally wrings the best performance out of you. Such a speech should appeal to your imagination, your heart, and your sense of the dramatic so that you feel compelled to "climb inside" the sentences and explore the lattice of subtle emotional and conceptual connections the writer first forged when communing with his muse. Only when you have such an intimate and powerful relationship with a speech will you have even a chance of bringing it to life during a performance.

The Script

How long does it take to write a monologue?

Words, as is well known, are great foes of reality.
—Joseph Conrad

How long it takes depends on a lot of things—the person writing, her work habits, the desired length of the monologue, and also how much editing she is prepared to do. I know someone who once wrote a monologue in a weekend, and it was quite good. I also know someone who spent four years writing and editing a monologue, and she still wasn't happy with it even when she finally performed it. For myself, when I write a forty-five-minute monologue it usually takes between six months and a year to distill all the things I want to talk about down to a manageable size and then severely edit it.

As with most art making, a monologue is like a nylon stocking, a supremely elastic phenomenon uniquely capable of expanding and contracting depending upon how much of yourself you want to put into it. In the end, I suggest you be less concerned with how *long* you want it to be and more concerned with how *good* you want it to be.

If I am a strong performer, is my script really that important?

That's a little like asking a two-person skating team, "If one of you is particularly strong and graceful, does it matter how good your partner is?" Of course it does. They're partners! And the relationship between your script and your performance is no different. If you are a weak performer, no script, no matter how stellar, will save the show. Likewise if you have a weak script, a brilliant performer will

Grampa Looked His Age

not be able to salvage it. Certainly it would be more interesting to watch the wonderful performer perform the weak script than vice versa (which is why they call it a "performing art"), but if at all possible you want your monologue to feature a strong performance *and* a strong script.

Your script, however, is your true beginning. It sets the parameters of your eventual performance. Or to put it another way, the script is the fuel for your performance, and it is with that and that alone that you will attempt to "burn" onstage. You can take to the stage with an armful of dry logs soaked in gasoline or a mere handful of limp, damp twigs. It's up to you.

Is there an ideal length for a monologue?

There is only one time when it is essential to awaken. That time is now.
—Azuki

The ideal length can be anywhere from fifteen minutes to an hour and a half. Shorter than that, and it's more of a rant. Longer than that, and you will run a very real risk of the audience finding you, frankly, tiresome if not actually dull. As always, it is better to leave them wanting more than to leave them wishing you had given them less.

But keep in mind that it takes even the most attentive of people a little while to "climb into your head." Even if your opening few minutes are especially effective (as I hope they are!), audience members are still becoming accustomed to the performance space, settling their bodies, and focusing their minds. This is why I usually suggest you write a monologue at least thirty minutes in length. Give yourself and your audience a chance to "meet."

You also may want to also ask yourself if one day you would like to produce your monologue for television. If so, it should be a minimum of forty minutes so that the producers and editors have enough to play with for a half-hour show.

How do I begin writing it?

Knowing others is wisdom, knowing yourself is enlightenment.
—Lao-tzu

As with most beginnings, beginning to write a monologue is less mysterious than you might think. You begin by beginning. I know, it sounds like a decidedly cute and empty answer, but the point I'm trying to make is: don't sweat it. Don't intimidate yourself by thinking, "Oh, my god, somehow I've got to write forty minutes of interesting, imaginative, and engaging things to say!" Hemingway referred to the blank page as "the white bull," beautifully capturing the daunting prospect of filling even a single white page with inspired prose. But there is no secret to beginning a writing project, and in fact, there are as many different ways to begin writing as there are writers.

Here's what I do. First, I try to pay attention to what's going on inside me; be aware of both my thoughts and my feelings. Then whenever a thought or feeling strikes me as particularly interesting (or at least relatively!), I force myself to scribble it down on a scrap of paper, a matchbook, a leather boot, or whatever is handy. I say "I force myself" because sometimes that's exactly what it takes. Push yourself. So whether it's a thought about love, death, television, past relationships, mammals, circus clowns, or brightly painted thimbles, if I think other people might find it interesting, stirring, insightful, funny, or even just clever, I jot it down.

This is an important part of being a writer: honoring your thoughts. Taking them seriously. So try to get in the habit of writing down observations, thoughts, feelings, poems, dreams, and so on. Not in the spirit of, "Everything I think and feel is pure genius," but rather, "Everything I think and feel is part of me, and I am part of the human race, and perhaps others will find such thoughts and feelings to be of value." See a Zen connection here? The premise that truth never exists in isolation, and that any one person's truth is necessarily a part of all our lives, reflects the Buddhist belief in the essential interconnectedness of all living things.

Then when I want to begin working on a new monologue, I just start going though this or that pile of notes. It's great therapy, sorting through a lush collection of your own quirky musings—both very personal and very "centering" at the same time. Usually as I reread the notes, I find that a few themes emerge, and based on those themes I begin to sort the notes into various smaller piles. I then take the next small step toward an actual script by sitting at my computer and expanding upon these loosely gathered notes. I must admit, few things give me greater satisfaction than tossing yet another small scrap of paper into the wastebasket, having dutifully included some thought into the first draft of a script.

And remember, this *is* only the first draft. Now's the time to follow your hunches and write whatever sounds good, engaging, or just plain interesting. Don't try to judge or evaluate it. Instead, have the faith, courage, and humility just to sit down and write. The evaluation part comes later. For now, just tell yourself you are trying to generate a "heap of words," which later you will artfully sculpt into something tight, economical, and well paced.

IS IT TRUE THAT OUT OF THE MOUTHS OF BABES OFTEN COME PROFOUND STATEMENTS?

Not quite. In my experience, out of the mouths of babes often come loud cries, a great deal of spit, and torrential rivers of undigested food. Not a pretty sight. Nor especially profound.

Should I try to include any other talents I may have in my monologue?

In the beginner's mind there are many possibilities, in the expert's mind there are few.

—Achaan Chaa

Whether you are an amateur juggler, an excellent archer, a magician, or able to eat an obscene amount of strudel, it is almost always a good idea to try somehow to include any of your talents in your monologue. For your first few monologues, especially, this is a good idea for two reasons.

First, by including an activity you have done hundreds of times before, you provide a few moments during the monologue where you are apt to be more comfortable and at ease. On some unconscious level, your psyche can look forward to a state of familiarity and control, which in turn will help you relax and stay focused. And second, an audience almost always appreciates anything that makes a theatrical performance that much more interesting or watchable. Of course, to distort and twist the natural flow of your monologue to accommodate two minutes of irrelevant tap dancing (and frankly, when isn't tap dancing irrelevant?) would be a mistake. But as always, the challenge is to write a monologue that, while staying focused and well paced, at the same time enables you to express and include as much of yourself as possible. Remember, profound sharing is about inclusion, not exclusion.

How do I choose a subject for my monologue?

Don't choose your subject. Let it choose you. In other words, ask yourself what moves or excites you. What subject or theme do you feel strongly about? Animal rights? Chocolate ice cream? Group therapy? The music of Sweden's supergroup Abba? And I assure you, you do feel extremely passionate about at least a handful of subjects, though it isn't always easy to know which ones these might be. But choose the theme or themes for your monologue very carefully, for it is from these first choices that all else will follow—the script, the marketing, the rehearsals, and the performances. Your passion for whatever theme(s) you choose will have to carry you through weeks or even months of work and preparation. And then, when it comes time to actually perform, this passion will once again serve as the fuel for your performances. The goal is to establish a relationship with your script that burns not only brightly, but long as well.

It's also always a good idea to write about what you *know* and have good reason to believe your audience will *care about*. For centuries writers have suggested to others, "Write about what you know," in the belief that a writer will be able to bring much more authority, insight, and detail to a subject with which he is extremely familiar than to a subject of which he has only a passing knowledge. So ask yourself, What do I know? All too often we presume that the activities with which we fill our days are uninteresting or boring to others. But believe me, there are no boring jobs, thoughts, or activities—only boring ways of perceiving and expressing them! Being a camp counselor or a gas station attendant or a homemaker or even an insurance salesman are all utterly fascinating ways of spending one's time . . . if only you have the eyes to see it and the words to express it. So beware of a pessimistic or dismissive view of the things you know and do. Trust me, not only do you know a great deal, but all that you know has the potential to be fascinating to others if it is presented in the right way.

And what is this "right way"? One important part is to present what you know with an unblinking eye toward what others likely will find interesting. Let's take an activity typically considered to be supremely dull, the scourge of stamp collecting. Okay, so maybe not everyone will find a monologue about ordering stamps from a catalog, waiting for them in the mail, and then finally adding them to a personal collection especially interesting. But what about a stamp collector's love of color or obsession with the political events surrounding the commissioning of a stamp, or even lust for an especially rare stamp? What, after all, are some of the possible psychological ingredients behind such an insular hobby? These are precisely the kinds of things people not only find interesting but would be willing to pay money to hear and watch a performer explore. So even as you ask yourself, What do I know and feel strongly about? *also* ask, What do people care about? I promise you, wherever those two spheres overlap, an extremely effective monologue awaits. (Incidently, if you still doubt the potential drama involved in collecting stuff, read John Fowles's brilliant book *The Collector.*)

WAS DR. SEUSS A COMMIE?

I very much doubt it, though he did write a lot of books that, while seeming to teach young children about the world, probably only ended up confusing a lot of them. After all, just how much really practical advice can you wring out of a statement like "One fish, two fish, red fish, blue fish"? Methinks the good doctor may well have been sampling his own wares.

Can you give me any tips on writing?

Zen is a way of liberation, concerned not with discovering what is good or bad or advantageous, but simply what is.

—Alan Watts

When writing, remember that simple is better. Simple also tends to be more powerful and, for the most part, much more difficult. But try your best to speak your truth as plainly as possible. Of course, it would be wonderful if you could speak your truth and express your unique perspective on this life in phrases both beautiful and memorable. But I assure you, unless you are among the rarest of writers, writing a script consisting of phrases that are honest and uncluttered will be more than enough of a challenge.

Also, don't edit until it is time to edit. Start off by letting your creative voice fly fast and furious (say *that* three times fast!). Ideally you want to get in the habit of wearing "two caps," that of the creator and the editor. Not that editing isn't creative, but I imagine both acts, though intimately connected, as being two different sides of the same coin. When you're wearing the creator's cap, focus on *expression* and let your unique and uninhibited voice come bubbling forth in an all-forgiving stream of consciousness. Then, when wearing the editor's cap, focus on *communication*. Dot the i's, cross the t's, and be an analytical, contemplative, second-guessing S.O.B. Being able to perform both functions with skill and insight is absolutely essential.

And be sure to write your monologue mostly in the first person. Writing a monologue in the third person is a little like using a violin bow to stir a pot of soup. You certainly can do it, but the bow is really much better suited to other activities. A monologue is about *you*. Certainly you can talk about your grandfather, your fear of flying, or your love of bowling (if you insist!), but never forget that those subjects and themes are mere vehicles, a means to an end—that end being the revelation of you.

Another technique you may want to follow is that of writing more about your feelings than about your thoughts. And write more about things that have happened or are happening to you, rather than about things that you believe may happen to you sometime in the future. As fascinating as the future can be, it is seldom as engaging as the past or present. Not only are past and present events somehow more real for most people, but such events tend to provide you as a performer with more emotional fuel than future imaginings.

And finally, when it comes to writing your monologue, the more intimate the better. Nothing is "too personal" or "too private" in a monologue. That would be like saying certain colors in a painting are "too vivid." It can be frightening to be very personal or intimate, especially in front of a group of strangers with whom you have established very little trust. In such moments, we can be afraid nobody in the crowd will be able to relate to our experiences, or that we will seem overly self-indulgent, or even that we might offend someone in the audience. And of course, we will commonly feel too exposed and vulnerable, and even fear that perhaps they will dislike us for who we "really" are.

But in such tense moments, remember these simple truths. The audience does not know you, and probably never really will, no matter how much of yourself you have the courage to share. So if they choose to dislike something, it is not *you* they dislike. It is just an extremely limited perspective of you. Also, remain mindful of the fact that your truth is not separate from theirs, and in sharing yours, you are enlightening us all. Care about their enjoyment, but not about their opinions. Have faith and be strong. Believe.

What if I'm a poor speller?

Fortunately, because a monologue is primarily an oral performance, your spelling abilities are of little consequence.

HOPELESS ROMANTIC

How should I begin my monologue?

The present moment is a powerful goddess.

—Goethe

I remember once hearing someone say, "Beginnings are extremely important, for it is from them that everything else follows." The first words, sentences, and paragraphs of your monologue do a great many things. They give the audience a first impression of you as both a performer and writer. They also set the tone of your monologue and establish an initial rhythm and subject matter.

As the writer, you want the first lines to be engaging, intriguing, funny—something, anything, that makes a definite, clear impression on the audience. These first lines literally "set the stage" for the rest of your monologue. And as the performer, you want the first lines to transport both you and your audience to whatever emotional realm you have in mind (sadness, excitement, and so on). "Get them on the bus"—the sooner, the better.

Does my monologue have to be funny?

Certainly not. Nor does it have to be especially sad, dramatic, exciting, suspenseful, sexy, or poetic. In fact, the question isn't so much whether your monologue has to be any of these things in particular, as whether it is *consistently engaging*. Think about those two words for a moment. The idea of consistency is pretty straightforward, meaning that your monologue has at least one relatively uniform quality about it, one that is present for much of its duration. But what does it mean to be "engaging"? It means, in a word, *stimulating*.

And how do you achieve this? By being funny or sad or anything else that the audience will find interesting! It's a matter of means and ends. Humor, tragedy, sex, and suspense are all only means to an end—tools, if you will. Your job is to use them as effectively as possible to keep your audience interested and, ideally, caring. And Lord knows there are countless ways to achieve this end. The question is, at what ways are you particularly adept? If you are funny, fine. If not, no great loss, assuming, that is, that you are comfortable being poetic or dramatic or tragic. But bear this in mind: a monologist is just one person, and if you are going to have the guts even to *attempt* to hold an audience's interest for thirty minutes, let alone an hour, you had better be willing to try a great many things. Once again, look to the masters of this craft. Practitioners such as Spalding Gray, Sandra Bernhard, and Eric Bogosian take their audiences on emotional and intellectual roller-coaster rides as they share their unique perspectives. And all while being—you guessed it—consistently engaging.

How should I edit my script?

First, cut your least favorite parts. I realize you perhaps had your heart set on a fifty-minute monologue, but trust me, a forty-minute monologue can often be a much, much better monologue. Especially if it's not bogged down with sections that the performer doesn't even really like! If in doubt, cut it out. When I'm working on a monologue, I always tend to start with way too much material. But to me, that's the fun, having all this interesting stuff to choose between and then arrange and rearrange.

Second, keep your favorite parts. You know, the parts you think are especially clever or funny or emotionally powerful. The audience may not feel about them the same way you do, but the parts you personally feel most strongly about are also probably the parts you will be able to perform most effectively—and an effective performance is the ultimate goal of any monologue script. Also, make sure you have spaced these "favorite parts" throughout your monologue rather than just lumped them all together near the beginning or end. A lost audience is never easy to get back, so don't lose them in the first place!

When you are finally finished editing, you have a script consisting of sections that, if you had to cut even one, you

ROMANTIC BUTCHER

would have a hell of a time deciding which would go. That's the sign of, if not a great script, at least a great *relationship* between a script and a performer. And that passionate and respectful relationship is really what you have been trying to create all along. Only then are you truly ready to begin rehearsing.

WHY DO THEY CALL IT "RUSH HOUR" WHEN THE TRAFFIC MOVES SO SLOWLY?

I have no idea.

Does every word of my monologue have to be scripted?

> *Zen aims at freedom, but its practice is disciplined.*
> —Gary Snyder

Another way of asking this question is, Can I improv or riff lines off the top of my head? Not only can you, but many monologuists come up with some of their best stuff that way. Of course, much of writing is about trying to be as clear, economical, descriptive, honest, and engaging as possible. And there's no question that sometimes it seems to take an awful lot of work, writing again and again, to arrive finally at a clear expression of a simple, powerful truth. So there is definitely a power to scripted material.

But there is also a power to the spontaneous, a power both the performer and the audience can *feel*. Many monologuists try to train themselves to trust both themselves and their audiences enough to riff when the mood takes them. For example, let's say at one point in your monologue you want to talk about eating watermelon and how you always associate it with the summer you worked as a rodeo clown in Connecticut. Fine, so write and edit a section of your monologue on that subject. However, as you find yourself delivering those lines onstage, coaxing yourself to imagine and even relive those hot summer days as a red-nosed freak dodging bull horns, grant yourself the psychological room to toss in whatever else comes to mind.

Rather than trying to control it, *go with it!* Certainly a well-written monologue tends to have a desired rhythm and a variety of carefully balanced recurring themes that you must remain true to. But at the same time, always try to allow yourself the freedom to speak your mind and share your heart on a subject, to find new and fresh things in a stream of words and images you have waded through a hundred times before. In this sense, no scene or story is every truly finished or "done." Stay open to vivid new details and vital spontaneous revisions! Let the presence of an interested audience inspire you to explore yourself and the moment.

How can I ensure that my monologue is stimulating?

Aim for quality and variety. Do a variety of things, and to the best of your abilities, do them well. I don't mean that throughout your monologue you should juggle bowling balls, fry eggs, recite Inuit poetry, and knit really itchy wool sweaters. In fact, there are many ways of expressing variety onstage while spending the entire hour calmly seated in a chair with your hands folded in your lap. Think about it. From one moment to the next you can vary subject matter, emotion, characterization, delivery, clothing, lighting, sound, and so on. Vary what you will, and as always let your aptitudes and passions be your guide. But when writing and performing your monologue, be sure to keep this crucial idea of variety in mind. It is one of the keys to keeping an audience's interest, without which your performance is doomed.

What about swearing?

Control your emotion or it will control you.

—Chinese adage

Again, it's a matter of personal taste and your objectives. But whether or not you decide to use especially provocative words, you should certainly ask yourself *why*. If you swear a lot offstage, I suspect you might do well to include at least a little swearing onstage, for the sake of both honesty and naturalness. I certainly swear from time to time offstage, and so I have often chosen to include a *small* amount of swearing onstage—but only during moments when I want to convey extreme anger or frustration. For me, swearing is a communication tool like any other, to be used purposefully and with restraint.

On the other hand, no matter how often you swear offstage, if you don't think you will feel comfortable swearing in front of a hundred strangers (including your grandmother, Father Muldowney, and your fiancée's parents), then I suggest you don't. But as with all art making, over time you must learn to distinguish between a discomfort that indicates a personal unnaturalness or even a creative wrongness and a discomfort that merely indicates an uncertainty or challenging newness.

What is a good title for a monologue?

Something short and relevant. As always, try to capture both people's attention and their imaginations. And remember, since you are going to use flyers, posters, and perhaps even a program to promote your show, the title must look at least as good as it sounds. For example, a title like *I* is certainly to the point, but maybe a bit dry, while the title *My Mind Is Like a Hot Fudge Sundae Being Eaten by a Three-Hundred-Pound Man Wearing Polyester Slacks and No Shirt* is probably a tad too long. Ask yourself, What is the predominant theme or topic of my monologue? and then brainstorm around that. Narrow it down to three or four of your favorites, and then you may want to consider doing what I do when it comes down to making such "final creative picks." I figure, hell, I like all of my "finals" for different reasons, so any of them really will do. But how then to choose between them? I don't. I let other people choose for me! I approach a few friends and anyone else who I think might typically reflect my monologue's potential target market and present them with a neatly typed out list of my four or five finalists.

I also give them a short blurb about the monologue, three or four sentences at most. Finally, I ask them simply to circle their favorite title. Then with any luck, after tallying the various choices, there will be a clear favorite. I go with that one and don't give it a second thought. Don't forget, I liked them all initially, and it's also always a good idea to include the influence of others in a communications project. (Which is precisely what a monologue is!)

Once while waiting in line at the grocery store I was flipping through one of those trashy little newspapers, and I read that some people are actually terrified of Christmas! Is this true?

Many more people are frightened by Christmas than will openly admit it. There's just something about the high-pitched songs, the deep red of Santa's suit, and all that "sneaking down the chimney" that strikes an anxious chord in the collective unconscious. Also, all that stuff about Saint Nick "knowing when you're sleeping, knowing when you're

awake, knowing if you've been bad or good, so be good for goodness' sake" smacks a little too much of Big Brother.

Interestingly, studies of the fear known as "santaclaus-trophobia" suggest that approximately 18 percent of the population become extremely agitated even *thinking* about spending an extended period of time trapped in a closet with an overweight, bearded, and inexplicably cheery gift giver. Then of course there's the cloud of anxiety surrounding presents—packages containing God knows what, and yet you are socially obliged to accept even the most inappropriate and disconcerting offering with a glowing smile. Truly, 'tis the season to be frightened.

Can I perform someone else's monologue?

An actor is, primarily, a philosopher. And the audience understands him as such.

—David Mamet

Certainly, though of course only if you have the author's permission. In fact, performing someone else's script is an especially good idea if you want to focus strictly on the performance aspects of the monologue form. Of course, you will undoubtedly perform another artist's monologue in quite a different way than originally imagined when the script was written. But that's the entire point: to bring to it an expression only you can bring. *Remember, as important as it is, the script is little more than the wick. The individual performer supplies the dynamite.*

Though it's certainly valid to perform a monologue written by another, many monologuists feel that the self-exploration and self-revelation inherent in the monologue form are ultimately best served when you perform your own words. Writing a monologue is a form of self-analysis. Like all art, it is a means of holding a mirror up to yourself and asking, How do I really feel or think about this or that? Or about me? Or about being human? The answers to such questions yield a script. Your script.

Later comes the performance, during which you share these thoughts and feelings with the audience. In this way, the monologuist first moves from thoughts and feelings to words (the script), and then moves from words to actions (the performance). And there are so many wonderful things to learn and explore during *both* processes! So though it's fine to perform the works of others, I urge you to listen to and encourage your own unique voice by writing your own script.

JUST HOW ACCURATE ARE THE PREDICTIONS FOUND IN FORTUNE COOKIES?

I can't say for sure, but for years I have been eating at the same Chinese restaurant, and I swear that at the end of the meal I always get a cookie with the exact same fortune in it: "Soon you be very sick." And stranger still, it's always right!

3

The Promotion

How can I promote my monologue?

There is no limit to the number of ways you can promote your show. But it is always a good idea whenever marketing anything to first ask yourself, Who is my target market? Obviously you want to get word of your monologue to theatrically minded people who regularly attend live performances. But perhaps you can be even more specific depending upon the *theme* of your monologue. If it's about being married for a long time and raising a family, older people are perhaps your ideal market. Or if your monologue is about coming out of the closet, then you may want to consider putting up flyers in gay or lesbian bars. If your show's about growing up as an athlete, target sports fans. If it's about your pet mouse, what about going to the park and handing out flyers to animal lovers walking their dogs or putting up a poster in a nearby pet shop? Keep asking yourself, Where is my audience? What do they do, and where do they frequent?

Also, what about putting an ad in a neighborhood newspaper? Or if that's too expensive, how about just spending an afternoon raiding newspaper boxes in the neighborhood where you plan to perform and stuffing your flyers into the middle of each paper? Seriously. You would be better off doing this with a weekly paper rather than a daily, in that it will give people more time to find your flyer (and won't they be impressed!). At the very least you can change the message on your answering machine: "Hi, I'm not home right now. But I'm presenting my monologue *My Night with Abe Vigoda* at the Periwinkle Theatre next week. Show-times are . . . "

But my favorite PR tool is probably the humble postcard. Yes they cost more than flyers, but considering how professional they look and how many different ways they can be effectively used, I think they're well worth the expense. With a fascinating photo on one side and all the vital info about your show on the other (place, times, phone number, and so on), a postcard is the perfect little promotional item to hand to friends or strangers on street corners, send to the media, stick in newspapers, pin to bulletin boards, leave in phone booths.

And be sure to call up everyone you can possibly think of (from the closest of friends to the vaguest of acquaintances) and tell them about your show. Don't be shy, you're in show business. I think you'll be pleasantly surprised by the response. Most people like an opportunity to do something a little different while supporting a friend at the same time. This too is a part of the profound sharing of the monologue experience. You ask for support from those around you, and they give it.

How do I go about getting media coverage?

One of the most common misperceptions of the popular media machine is that writers and editors call you. Ha. Yeah, right. Ha ha ha. It is to laugh. The fact of the matter is that though newspaper writers and editors are constantly looking for stories to print because they need a literally never-ending stream of newsworthy or interesting events, they won't contact you. *You* must call *them*. After all, every day they arrive at work to find a desk covered in mail and a phone swollen with messages. Why should they bother calling possible "stories" when they merely have to choose among the ones lying on their desk?

This is why it is up to you, first, to convince them that your monologue is *newsworthy*. This can be difficult when you are just starting out, but once you get a few articles, a couple of mentions, or even just a single glowing quote (hopefully from an "impressive" someone), you will gain

FUNERAL DIRECTOR

some media credibility, and it will be easier to get some press for an upcoming performance. Easier, but seldom actually easy.

Keep one thing in mind: we live in a visually oriented culture. As a result, one of the most valuable things you can have in your press package is an arresting, professionally shot photograph. If you are serious about media coverage, this is absolutely essential. And don't have your friend take the photo. *Go to a professional.* Yes, it will cost a couple of hundred dollars, but I assure you it will be worth it. And be sure to go with a black-and-white shot, because that's the nature of the newspaper medium. Actually, if you can afford to have both a black and white *and* a color shot done, it's even better, just in case they want to run a few color pictures in their "weekend listings" section but don't have much to choose from. You just might get lucky.

And don't go with a dull "head shot" (who cares what you look like?). To promote *Contents under Pressure,* I used a photo of me standing in an alley with a large wooden vise clamped on my head. To add to the surreal feel of the photo, the photographer (Christopher Sankey, who—lucky for me—is not only my dear brother and a physician but also a professional hotshot photographer) took my picture with a fish-eye lens. The result was a picture both funny and memorable.

I suggest you think a great deal about the photo you want *before* the shoot date. Show up with a variety of shirts and at least two good ideas in mind, and then let the shutterbug do his or her thing. And again, make sure your photo ideas are relevant to your show. If your monologue is about crime, what about having your photo taken in a mock police lineup? Or if your monologue is about growing up on a farm, have your picture taken in a wheat field.

Do something—*anything*—different, interesting, and graphically bold. And be sure to keep it visually simple; if you are fortunate enough to have it run in a local paper, your shot may very well be reduced to the size of a postage stamp. So remember that the small details of the shot should not determine whether or not a reader "understands" the picture.

DID THAT WOMAN WHO ORIGINALLY "SOLD SEASHELLS DOWN BY THE SEASHORE" EVER GET INTO FRANCHISING?

I very much doubt it. I mean, considering that she chose to open her shop where people can walk along the beach and, at any time of the day or night, actually pick up shells *for free,* how many seashells do you think she really sold? Location, location, location! What's next? Selling twigs in a forest?

What is a press release?

This is a single page of information that you send to the newspapers and radio stations in the area where you will be performing. When writing this important piece of promotion, remember to be brief and matter-of-fact. Leave it to others to write the hyperbole. Media people receive dozens of notices and press releases every day, and if your release is not extremely direct, they will simply take a quick glance at it and toss it in their omnivorous trash cans.

Across the top of the page type PRESS RELEASE. Immediately below, type the title of your show, your name, the location of the show, and then below that the dates and times of the performances. Write a short paragraph (two or three sentences, not five or six!) telling a little bit about your monologue (its subject, some of the themes, the style, and so on). And if there are any "mixed medium" aspects to your monologue (slides, music) be sure to mention them. Finally, write a *few* sentences mentioning any interesting or relevant information about yourself. If your monologue is about being a bouncer in a bar and you actually have worked at several bars, mention that. If your monologue is about religion and you have a degree in theology, mention that. And of course, if you have any previous performance experience, be sure to mention this as well.

End your press release with a clear and friendly request for some "media support." I often write something like, "Thanks for your time, and I would certainly appreciate any support your publication can lend my upcoming local performances." Be sure to include your phone number: "For more information or to set up an interview please call..." When it comes to mailing out press releases, remember that it is always much better to send stuff to an *individual* than to a faceless department. So be sure to go to the trouble of calling up the various publications to get the names (and correct spellings!) of the appropriate people, that is, listing and entertainment editors.

If your monologue is about a theme or subject that itself may have particular relevance to a specialty newspaper, be sure to send them a press release. For example, many cities have newspapers targeted toward specific segments of the population—the black community, gays and lesbians, computer programmers, bicycle thieves, pudding aficionados, and so forth. If your monologue deals explictly with issues relevant to such publications and their readers, they often will be quite enthusiastic about doing a story.

Should I enclose a gimmick with my press release and photo?

No object is mysterious. The mystery is your eye.

—Elizabeth Bowen

I have heard many media people say they prefer not to receive a gimmick with a press release. And yet, I admit I have had great success with gimmicks! So I just keep using them, even though I'm sure they may rub one or two people the wrong way. As always, it is probably not so much a matter of *what* you do, but *how* you do it. A silly, inappropriate, or unoriginal gimmick is not only a waste of time and money but a waste of a "communications opportunity." But a clever, funny, or imaginative gimmick, one that speaks of both thought and quality, can be a memorable catalyst for further contact.

The first thing I look for in a gimmick is something that the recipient is likely to want to *keep* rather than throw away. Over the years, I have used a wide range of promotional gimmicks—including rubber penguins, high-quality candy (stuff you wouldn't find at the corner store!), origami figures, jazz CDs, small plastic nuns, and even ice cream parlor gift certificates. Be imaginative and try not to be cheap. Your goal is to appear as if you *could have* spent more money, but for discretion's sake you instead chose a simple, fun, cool, and imaginative token. And try to think of the money you spend on promotion as a long-term investment. If such gimmicks increase your chances of obtaining even a single small article in a local weekly newspaper, the effort can generate a surprising amount of interest. Not to mention the fact that you have another "piece" for your promo kit!

The second thing I look for in a gimmick is (yet again) relevancy. If your show's about working as an auto mechanic, then tiny toy wrenches, perhaps even on key chains, make a great deal of sense. Jumbo chocolate bars or baskets of fruit do not. A truly relevant gimmick aids your communication by implicitly supporting the theme of your show, taking the edge off any possible "bribe" implications and at the same time being an example of the excellence of your communication abilities. This in turn sets the tone for future communications to come.

What about newspaper articles?

Newspaper articles are among my favorite media tools because, unlike radio and even television interviews, a newspaper article is cheap to reproduce and makes for the perfect addition to a promo package. Newspaper coverage roughly breaks down into three different degrees of "focus." First there's the "brief mention," either in a larger article or perhaps in a "what to do this weekend" column. Then there's the "small review." This is much better in that it is more ink on the page and hopefully will give you something to reproduce for your promo package. And finally there's the "feature." The feature is a dream come true—an entire article (big or small—who cares?!) all about you and your show. Immediately copy and mail (or fax) it to every important decision maker you can possibly think of.

Perhaps the trickiest part of getting some newspaper coverage is trying to figure out the best time to send a particular writer your package. In my experience, writers like to receive promotional stuff between two and three weeks before an event. Though timing may not be everything, in the world of mass media it counts for a great deal.

How can I use a newspaper article to further promote myself?

As your career progresses, you should be gathering a list of names and addresses of agents, producers, and so on. Then whenever you get some media coverage, be sure to send a copy to these decision makers along with a short note, such as "just to keep you up to date." If at all possible, always include a sincere and personal line or two with anything you send anyone. It goes a long way toward making the recipient feel personally acknowledged.

A newspaper review or magazine article (even from a tiny, unknown publication) is also the perfect thing to photocopy and hand out to promote your show. Be sure to print clearly the place and times of any upcoming performances on the page, along with a contact number. And might I suggest that when photocopying, you use something other than a white paper stock. In your offical promotional package you always should use only white stock, because agencies and the media routinely make several copies of whatever they receive (white copies better). But for handouts or even press releases, a little color lends cachet to your show. This is especially so during a festival, where the majority of the handouts people receive are on boring, cheap white paper. Spend a few extra bucks and make a better impression.

And finally, don't think you have to have an entire article written just about you and your show before you have something to hand out. Magazine and newspaper writers commonly review several plays in a single article, especially during festival reviews. In such cases I suggest you cut out the paragraph about your show, as well as the heading of the article (including the writer's byline and the newspaper's name and date). Then have these elements *enlarged* on a photocopier. And finally, neatly lay out the enlarged heading, the paragraph, and the newspaper's name and date on a single sheet of 8 x 11 paper. Voilà! A clear, effective flyer. My thinking is, Why promote other shows when I'm the one paying for the photocopying and taking the time to hand out flyers?

What if I get a bad review?

> *Whoever makes good progress in the beginning has all the more difficulties later on.*
>
> —Eugen Herrigel,
> *Zen in the Art of Archery*

Learn from it what you can, and then *forget about it*. As the expression goes, "Everyone's a critic." We each have our prejudices, preferences, and points of view, and I do not believe any of them are more "valid" or "important" than any others. However, sometimes someone else's perspective can be, if not enlightening, at least insightful. The key is to try to stay open to positive criticism (criticism shared in a supportive manner with an eye toward growth) and do what you can to ignore negative criticism. Some stuff is constructive, some destructive.

Even as you nurture your creativity and the gift of your unique voice, so too is it your responsibility to *protect* it, especially from those who would harm, confuse, or weaken it. But try to stay open to the "two cents" of others, while never forgetting that it is nothing more than the "two cents" of another ignorant mortal steeped in his own myopic prejudices and unconscious agendas.

What if I get a good review?

Do not blindly believe what others say. See for yourself what brings contentment, clarity, and peace. That is the path for you to follow.
—Angarika Sujata

In many ways, this presents an even greater danger than a bad review. A positive review is always nice for your ego and can certainly draw more people to your shows, but again it is only the "two cents" of another person. Try not to take such praise too much to heart, if only because you will be setting yourself up for an even bigger disappointment when you get a bad review. And believe me, sooner or

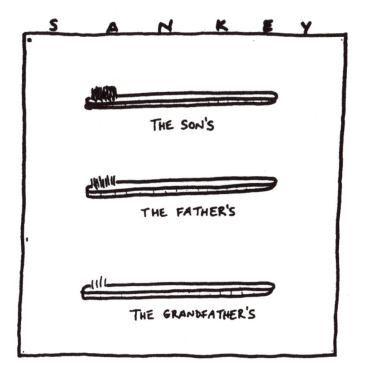

THE SON'S

THE FATHER'S

THE GRANDFATHER'S

later *everyone* gets a bad review. So learn what you can from both good and bad reviews, clip out the good ones and add them to your promotional package, and then forget them all and keep your mind focused on the real task at hand: the nurturing of your own creative voice.

PEOPLE SAY IT IS BETTER TO GIVE THAN RECEIVE. IS THIS TRUE?

It depends. For example, if you enjoy a good steak, done medium rare with a dash of peppercorn sauce and maybe some fried potatoes and mixed greens, and one day you find yourself sitting in front of just such a meal with a loudly gurgling tummy, then to hand it over (potatoes and all) to a starving family of five seated nearby is utter foolishness. On the other hand, if you recieve something in the mail, for example a soiled mitten, then it makes a great deal more sense to generously give it away in the spirit of Christian love. Perhaps even to the family of five. As always, sharing is the key.

What about radio interviews?

These are often easier to get then you might think, but as always, you have to do your homework. Your goal is to find both a radio station and a host suitable for your style of performance and monologue subject matter. Ask yourself, What is the radio station's target audience? After all, though any and all media experience can only benefit you, you want to promote your monologue to listeners who might actually come out and see it. In other words, if you're doing an upbeat, manic monologue on the four hard years you spent turning tricks while in prison, trying to land an interview with a mellow, pun-loving host on a radio station targeted toward listeners aged sixty-plus and featuring "the golden sounds of the Big Band Era" may not be such a good idea. Choose your host and station wisely.

Once you've got a short list of possible stations, mail some information about yourself and your monologue to the appropriate person. Then follow up with a phone call and offer to do a brief interview *any time they want*. To prepare for the interview, select a few short excerpts from your monologue, stuff that is still powerful and engaging even when read out of the context of the entire monologue. Comedic passages are always a safe bet. Alternatively, songs, poems, and any "rants" on topical news items or popular culture also tend to go over quite well on radio. And be sure to bring a can of pop or bottle of water with you to the station. Your mouth may go dry, and not all radio stations will be sure to offer you a beverage.

How much should I charge for tickets to my show?

It ain't worth nothing if it ain't free.

—Janis Joplin

Well, perhaps you should consider *giving them away,* especially if you are a very inexperienced monologuist. After all, how sure are you that people will receive their money's worth? On the other hand, if you are renting a performance space or equipment, you understandably would like to recoup some of your costs, and so a nominal fee for a ticket might be a good idea. But keep in mind, apart from a handful of "big shows," most theatrical performances are not out to make a great deal of money. More often they have as their goal the thrill of performance and the joy of an appreciative audience (ideally while *losing* as little money as possible!). However, the good news is that, considering you are a "cast of one," you will get to keep 100 percent of any ticket sales or perhaps have to share them only with your director.

Speaking of which, unless your director is such a generous person that he or she has agreed to work for free, I would suggest that you pay your director a fixed fee rather than a percentage of ticket sales. Much of the director's work occurs before the first audience member ever shows up, so it's only fair.

Many monologues premiere at fringe festivals where a maximum ticket price is already set (often around seven or eight dollars), and so you will have very little say in the area of ticket prices. But if your monologue continues its run after the festival or even as the show becomes more polished and effective, you may well be justified in raising your ticket prices. After all, your show is now a stronger, "audience-tested" piece of theater.

However, most monologuists don't make a lot of money and do it for the satisfaction, personal growth, and creative challenge. Just think for a moment about the many things you do for "free": listening to music, talking with friends, having sex, and eating banana cream pie (sometimes all at the same time!). Most of these have no potential to make money, but instead have great *intrinsic* value. The arts, however, not only nurture self-growth and social communication but even have the potential to make some money, however little. And keep in mind, money is only something you can use *after* the task. During the experience, it is as if the money does not exist. In that sense, I suspect money can never truly justify or make sense of an action. Only personal satisfaction can do that.

IS A PENNY SAVED REALLY A PENNY EARNED?

If you have indeed saved a penny, it seems fair to say that, in a sense, you have "earned" the penny, the possession of the penny being the reward or payment for having not spent it. But let us not forget that we are in fact talking about a single penny. These days, what can you buy with a damn penny! And let's say you even doubled or tripled your efforts and went so far as to save two or even three pennies. What does it matter? We're still just talking about a few cents. Call it "earning" if you must, but either way, I would strongly suggest you put down your thesaurus and get to work making some real money! Trust me, this "penny" crap is a complete waste of time. Nowheresville.

Should I have a show program printed?

A program is always fun, though I don't think it's necessary to have it printed. Photocopying is just fine. The program should be brief and to the point, mentioning the title of the monologue, the name of the writer, performer, and director, and any other appropriate credits and thanks. It is also always a good idea to list any other dates and times you plan to perform your show.

But apart from these "information-based" aspects of the traditional program, there are other worthwhile things you can do with your program. Actually, don't think of it simply as a "program," but as yet another communication opportunity. Chances are, your program will be the first direct contact many people in the audience will have with the "theme" or theatrical intent of your monologue. As such, you may want to consider seriously reproducing an image, a short poem, or a narrative passage to gently "prime" the audience's collective perspective for your own individual perspective. Remember, many people will be sitting in the audience with "nothing to do" for at least a few minutes before your show begins. Don't waste this incredible opportunity! Make the most of it with a well-thought-out program.

How will I know when my monologue is ready to be seen by producers, agents, and other important decision makers?

> *Zen has no theory; it is an inner knowing for which there is no clearly stated dogma. It deemphasizes the power of the intellect and extols that of intuitive action.*
>
> —Joe Hyams

This is a tricky call; frankly, almost *any* time other people are interested in seeing you perform is a "good time," especially considering how rare such interest can sometimes be. But ideally, you want any individuals who can dramatically influence your career to see you perform under the best possible conditions—when you are completely comfortable with the script and are performing in front of a supportive, enthusiastic audience. So you may well want to consider performing your monologue in front of a crowd, any crowd, as many times as possible before inviting agents and producers to come out to see you. But again, even if they do come out, there's no guarantee that they will see you at your best.

For instance, I once performed my monologue *Borrowed Breath* during a festival, and as is often the case during festivals, some of my shows were scheduled during the evening and some during the afternoon. And of course, as fate would have it, some important producers came out to see me during my most poorly attended show. What fun! One o'clock on a rainy Wednesday afternoon, performing a (supposedly) comic monologue about death and dying for *six people,* two of whom just happen to be jaded television producers. I can assure you, it was an extremely long, extremely silent fifty minutes. And no, I never did hear back from the television people.

IS A CHOCOLATE DOUGHNUT A VITAMIN-ENRICHED, HIGH-PROTEIN SNACK SUITABLE FOR HEALTH-CONSCIOUS INDIVIDUALS?

Actually, no. Many people don't realize this, but doughnuts are not as healthy for you as say, broccoli. Or lima beans. Or zucchini. Or spinach. Or green peppers. Or even bananas. This is because while broccoli and many other vegetables and fruits are chock-full of vitamins and minerals, doughnuts consist mostly of sugar, fat, and bad karma. Truly Satan's snack food. But *man,* they're tasty!

What should I have in my promo kit?

In order of importance: (1) a brief description of your monologue; (2) photos; (3) newspaper articles, reviews, and any mentions; and (4) your bio, including educational and employment history and especially any background in performance and communications.

How do I promote myself to film and television producers?

First impressions last.

—Popular expression

One of the keys to self-promotion is to make sure your first impressions are as *strong* and as *memorable* as possible. And this applies to every aspect of your communication, whether it is your letterhead, a phone call, a performance, or an in-person meeting. So rather than trying to get the attention of a producer, agent, or newspaper columnist via persistent but lackluster communications, try instead fewer but more memorable contacts.

HAPPY BIRTHDAY

Even if you are an especially effective communicator, there's always a risk of overdoing it. The so-called follow-up call (typically made to thank a contact or make sure they have received the information you sent them) should be made only if you firmly believe it will work in your favor. Trust your intuitions. If you have doubts, they may be well-founded, and you will end up only annoying the contact. If they know who you are and what you are doing, they will contact you if they are interested.

But there *are* exceptions. A couple of years ago I wanted to catch the eye of a woman who was looking to produce several shows of stand-up comedy for television, and I did not want to be overlooked. So after "bumping into her" at an industry party, I made a point of sending her an obviously expensive plush toy. It was an elephant, to be exact, with a little note (handwritten on one of my postcards) saying, "Don't forget me!"

Why the elephant? First, I admit that the gender of the producer *did* influence my choice of a plush toy, but I realized that if I was going to send this influential person a stuffed animal, it was going to have to be one that instead of just being "cute and gentle" had an inherent strength. The elephant was also the perfectly poetic way for me to refer to the "don't forget me" theme, what with the pachyderm's legendary memory. In the end, it comes down to going with what feels right for you.

IF MOHAMMED WON'T GO TO THE MOUNTAIN, IS IT REALLY A GOOD IDEA TO BRING THE MOUNTAIN TO MOHAMMED?

I don't think so. Even small mountains with very little vegetation tend to be quite heavy and so the moving costs can be considerable. And who's going to pay for such a move? Certainly not Mohammed. He didn't even care enough about the mountain to be willing to visit it in the first place. So forget all the usual chat about moving large ancient land masses. Instead of the mountain, I suggest you bring Mohammed a nice bottle of wine. Nothing too fancy, but nothing too cheap either. Red or white, it makes no matter. But the higher the alcohol content the better. After a couple of glasses of high-octane hooch, good old Mohammed won't even remember the mountain.

What is a fringe festival, and how can I apply to one?

Many of the larger cities in the United States and Canada have annual "fringe festivals," usually lasting between four days and two weeks. During the festival a variety of alternative theatrical venues are made available to mostly nonprofessional groups of writers, actors, and directors. Some festivals accept applications on a first-come, first-served basis, while others do a random drawing to arrive at a final list of lucky applicants. Whatever the process, there is often a substantial application fee involved, but considering that these festivals tend to be very well promoted and attended, many participants make back enough money in ticket sales to cover at least their original investment.

For example, it cost me around $300 to enter my first fringe festival in Toronto. But I was guaranteed six shows, and at $5 a ticket I figured that I only had to have a total of sixty-five people attend my shows to break even. I told myself ten people per show was something I could do. And as it turned out, I did more than double that. For more information on fringe festivals, please refer to "Fringe Festivals," at the back of the book.

4

The Stage

Do I need to be standing on a stage to perform a monologue?

There are no holy places and no holy people, only holy moments, only moments of wisdom.

—Eido Tai Shimano

A theater setting is a focused, reverential space usually featuring good sound and sight lines, all of which inspire both performers and audiences alike. In such a space you also can control the entry and exit of the audience as well as the music and lighting.

You may not be able to afford a large theater, but most cities and towns are filled with fascinating places and spaces, many of which have strong theatrical potential for those with the imagination to *see it.* Hundreds of performers every year give wonderful shows in church basements, parks, tents, alleys, or even just standing on the street. Don't let economics and architecture defeat your theatrical vision! Imagine a monologue about the theme of transportation taking place in a subway car, even as an ever-changing audience gets on and off. Or how about delivering a monologue from a swing in the park? Or in a grocery store after hours? Dead-end streets, rooftops, front lawns, fire escapes, and even your own living room can all make for charming, manageable performance spaces. Be daring, be imaginative, and have fun!

Do I need to use a microphone?

The actor is onstage to communicate the play to the audience. That is the beginning and the end of his or her job.

—David Mamet

This is yet another choice completely dependent upon the personal taste, needs, and aesthetic of the individual performer. If you have performed in front of people only a few times and tend to get a little nervous and be soft-spoken, a microphone may not be a bad idea. A microphone might also be a good idea if you plan to perform in front of a particularly large audience. If there is even the slightest chance that, for whatever reason, your audience may not be able to easily hear your voice, then I suggest you definitely use a microphone.

Certainly your facial expressions and body movements are an important part of your performance, but when it comes to the monologue form, it is your *voice* that is far and away your most valuable and powerful communication tool. For this reason it must be conveyed effectively at any cost. Spalding Gray often uses a table microphone, delivering many of his monologues seated behind a table. There are, however, a variety of other microphones commonly available, including standing mics (what most stand-up comics use) and lapel mics that simply clip to your shirt collar with a small battery pack in your back pocket. But be warned, microphones are not inexpensive, even just to rent.

When I first performed my monologue *Contents under Pressure,* I decided to use a lapel mic, but instead of going with an expensive "wireless mic," I actually had the microphone cord running down through my shirt, down my pants, and out one pantleg to the wings of the stage. I saved a lot of money, and fortunately I spent much of the monologue seated, but I admit at times it was uniquely uncomfortable.

Also keep in mind the different *feel* a performance has if you decide to use a microphone instead of simply projecting your natural voice. Electronically conveying your voice certainly can increase volume and clarity, but depending upon the quality of the mic, you may well lose some of your

Unsportsmanlike Conduct

voice's more subtle qualities. A mic also definitely affects the essential *intimacy* of your voice. The mere presence of a mic also sends to the audience a message of "this is a performance," in contrast to the "just chatting" feel of a non-mic performance. As always, it's about weighing your practical options and artistic priorities and going with what best suits your abilities and the goals of your performance.

WHY IS IT DANGEROUS TO SMOKE IN BED?

I never understood this myself. We've all heard about someone being killed because they were smoking in bed and fell asleep, but how the hell does that work? I mean, I can't think of a more effective way of waking someone up than lighting their bed on fire. Think about it. A blazing fire tends to give off a fair bit of heat, smoke, light, and sound. I just can't see someone in a blazing bed rolling over and hitting the snooze button on their clock radio.

Should I use music?

Absolutely! I confess to a strong love of (and belief in) music. It not only hath charms to soothe the savage beast, but can be used elegantly in a monologue to achieve a wide range of goals. Music heard as people file into the space can set a tone for an entire monologue. Heard during a single scene, music can support the scene in a powerful implicit fashion. Music can even work wonders when it comes to smoothing the transitions between scenes.

I have such faith in music that, frankly, I sometimes have to restrain myself from *over*using it! And you don't necessarily need a professional sound system either. Even a cassette tape in a small portable player (started and stopped at the appropriate times by a friend) can add a surprising amount to a monologue. As always, make a point of experimenting. Have fun and don't be afraid to be too creative.

I also wouldn't be too concerned about the legal rights of the musicians whose music you decide to "borrow," unless of course you plan to record or produce your monologue for something other than a live situation, such as television. Then of course it's a whole different matter, both ethically and legally. However, if you do plan to use an artist's music in a live performance context, be sure to credit the artist in your program.

In *Contents under Pressure* I play a few of my own weird little melodies on an electric keyboard, but for *Borrowed Breath,* as people enter the theater I use a Tom Waits song to help set the tone. I performed the show only locally and gave him credit in the program, so I would like to think he wouldn't mind.

What about sound cues?

If you take care of each moment, you will take care of all time.
—Lao Tzu

Whether you are planning to have two sound cues or thirty, you always should make a point of recording each sound cue at the beginning of a *separate* tape. That way, with each cue on its own tape, whoever is handling your sound does not have to fiddle with any fast-forwarding or rewinding. Such things are always nerve-racking, and sooner or later will result in a sound cue that is mistimed or missed altogether, either of which can really throw off both performer and audience.

It's also important that you and whoever is working your sound figure out the *precise* sound levels of each tape. Nothing is more frustrating than to make an inspired music choice for a certain section of your monologue and then find yourself having to shout over it or lower your voice to a whisper so it can be heard. Each tape should of course also be clearly marked on the cassette box and on the tape itself. Electronic and stereo stores commonly sell carrying cases holding anywhere from five to fifteen cassettes, an ideal means of keeping the tapes ordered and accessible.

What about lighting?

Always a good idea, especially if you want the audience to be able to see you. And so the question isn't so much whether or not you should use light in your monologue, but *how* you should use it. You would do well to give this question a fair bit of thought because it can impact greatly the tone, clarity, and focus of your performance. Unfortunately, the question of lighting is often a last-minute consideration for inexperienced monologuists. If at all possible, when you've decided upon a performance venue, whether it's a large theater, a small neighborhood hall, or even your living room, begin rehearsing *in that space* as soon as possible. This will give you time to experiment with whatever lighting options the space offers.

And when experimenting, have someone stand in for you onstage (ideally wearing clothes similar to your performance attire) as you sit in a "typical seat" in the audience. Only then will you have a dependable idea of the lighting effects. And make no mistake, lighting is real magic. With a simple flick of a switch you can take the minds of the audience under the ocean, into a bonfire, high into the sky, or back into the womb—just by some thoughtful use of color and brightness.

The first time I staged a series of performances of *Contents under Pressure,* I was on a shoestring budget, but I was still able to use a general stage wash, a white spotlight, a red spotlight, and even a large hand-held flashlight! All of these effectively set a variety of tones, feels, and focuses during certain points in the monologue. As always, your goal is to stimulate the audience and keep them engaged. That is not to say you should try to use as many different lighting effects as possible, though you certainly should try to make the most creative and supportive use of whatever lighting equipment is at your disposal.

By "supportive" I mean that whatever you use in your monologue, be it a word in your script, a tie around your neck, a gesture of your hand, or a certain color of gel on a spotlight, should be consciously used only to serve the overall goal of your monologue. I've said it before, I'll say it again. If you are not sure about the addition of something to your monologue, be it a line or a light, it is usually better to drop it.

What about a specially designed set?

There are three different kinds of elements making up any performance environment: those that *aid* the performer in the creation of an intended experience, those that *impede* the performer in such an experience, and those that neither aid nor impede. For example, if you wanted to perform your monologue in your living room, which happens to have a large window facing a bus stop where people frequently gather, such a window may well impede the goals of your performance. On the other hand, if you have an aquarium in your living room, and your monologue makes various references to fish, water, or even themes of imprisonment, such an element in the performance space might well enhance the experience. As for elements that you deem to be neither impeding nor aiding, so-called neutral elements, omit them. This leaves greater opportunity for the more clearly effective elements to "speak."

I am not convinced that as a monologuist you necessarily have to spend a great deal of time and effort on complicated sets. Even in this matter, less tends to be more. But if you do choose to explore such technical avenues, I strongly urge you to seek professional advice, if not actual assistance. After all, when you write and perform your monologue, you are utilizing skills you employ every day: word choice, pacing, even talking to several people at the same time. In a sense, writing and performing a scripted monologue in front of fifty strangers is only a stretch (albeit a daunting one) of our everyday activities.

Set design is a whole other matter. If you decide not to seek experienced guidance, why not disregard sets altogether and simply put more time and energy into your script and performance? I assure you, there is always more work to be done in those areas. (And thankfully, more to be gained.)

WHY DO MIRRORS REVERSE OUR IMAGES HORIZONTALLY, BUT NOT VERTICALLY?

Wow. You really know how to ask 'em. Luckily I'm pretty sure I know the answer to even this complicated question. In a word, Satan. You see, the Dark One wants to distract our thoughts from the vertically oriented "heaven/hell" dichotomy and instead have us focus on more horizontal "east/west" imaginings, such as "boy, would I love to go to Great Britain for a pint." Keeping us distracted, the Destroyer of Souls realizes he dramatically increases the odds of us acting in a sinful manner. And considering that commercially produced mirrors exist largely in response to human vanity, a classic hot spot for sin, little wonder Beelzebub routinely works his dark magic through bathroom mirrors. Really quite simple, isn't it?

How about the use of slides?

Technical knowledge is not enough. One must transcend techniques so that the art becomes an artless art, growing out of the unconscious.
—Daisetz Suzuki

Projected images can be employed subtly to add ambient color or mood to a scene, or they can be used boldly as an explicit visual aid. In *Swimming to Cambodia,* Spalding Gray uses slides to lovely effect, and I have seen many monologuists use slides to display everything from maps to X rays. Such eye candy is almost always welcomed by an audience, but as with all technology it must be used with considerable craft and restraint.

With *Borrowed Breath* I wanted to establish a comedic tone (to balance the monologue's theme of death and dying) as early as possible. So even as the audience filed in to find their seats, I had a series of single-panel cartoons appear on a screen onstage. Each image was visible for ten to fifteen seconds, and then another would appear in its place. Several of the "dark and morbid" cartoons were funny enough to make members of the audience laugh out loud, going a long way toward establishing the monologue as humorous. This was absolutely essential if I wanted to avoid the risk of losing the audience's trust from the very beginning of this decidedly macabre monologue.

Slides, however, do present a number of technical challenges, all of which directly affect the overall theatrical experience. First, do you project your images from behind the screen or in front? Chances are you would rather conceal as much of the technology as possible, but perhaps you do not want to spend any more money than you absolutely have to, and back projection systems usually cost more. Then there is the matter of where to position the screen onstage. If you put it to one side of the stage (with you performing on the other), you have divided the focus of your

OUR FATHER WHO ART UNLEADED

stage. This arrangement can work in your favor, but you must manage such a division thoughtfully. However, probably the largest challenge a slide projector presents is that of sound. Most relatively inexpensive slide projectors are quite noisy due to both their small fan and the loud *clickity-click* they make with each changing slide.

I used the comic slides in *Borrowed Breath* not only as a teaser before the actual monologue, but also during the fifty-minute performance itself. Every few minutes I would have a new slide appear, either a cartoon or a simple, bold graphic in some way relevant to whatever I was at that point discussing. Unfortunately, several of the photos I originally had planned on using did not develop as well as I had hoped, so I immediately cut them out of the final production. Such is the art-making process.

IF A SINGLE CLOUD CAN HOLD UP TO TEN MILLION GALLONS OF WATER, WHY DON'T CLOUDS FALL TO EARTH?

Sheer vanity. Oh sure, on some unconscious level most clouds realize they are decidedly bloated and a tad unwieldy, but clouds love to put up a good front and move around as if they're dainty little things. But take my word for it, every second they remain floating in the air costs them dearly, and by the end of the day most clouds are completely exhausted by the effort to stay airborne. This is precisely why you'll see far fewer clouds in the sky at night than during the day. First chance they get, they barrel off to some secluded corner of the world and gorge themselves on cool streams and deep green ponds. Then it's up at the crack of dawn to begin daintily parading themselves as if they are something other than the Winnebagos of the air. Such is vanity.

What about blackouts onstage?

Blackout is a lighting term indicating a complete shutting off of the stage lights. It is typically used at the end of a scene or the entire play. It's a kind of visual transitional aid, its semantic equivalent being, "And then…" As effective as blackouts can be, this technique is frequently overused. Be warned.

In most professional spaces absolute blackout (including any lights in the audience) is frowned upon and usually illegal, as it presents a hazard to any audience member who either has to suddenly leave the theater or perhaps merely find her way back to her seat after a trip to the washroom. So it is a good idea for you, as the writer and performer (and perhaps even the director), to keep in mind that any blackout you desire will not be complete.

What about stagehands and assistants?

And if we are lost, then we are lost together.

—Blue Rodeo

What are friends for? I bet you can dig up a friend or two who is interested enough in both you and the theater to be glad to help out. But choose your assistants very carefully. You are asking them to do nothing less than be intimately involved in your creative quest (even if you need them only to move two chairs and hit Play on the tape recorder). The last thing you want to do is have someone hanging around during rehearsals who turns out to be an opinionated, even negative, influence.

Here, then, are the four qualities I look for in an assistant or stagehand. First, positivity. Believe me, whether your first performance goes well or not, you are going to want to have as many "positive vibes" around you as possible. Second, responsibility. An assistant who is always late for rehearsals or cannot be completely counted on to take care of this or that is an absolute liability in the theater. Third, a secure ego. I have seen monologuists get into repeated arguments with an assistant. I believe it was at least partly because the assistant was (on some level) uncomfortable with being just that, *an assistant.* Onstage, your task is to try to woo your muse, to be an inspired performer. And your assistant's job is to assist you in that matter. There *is* a pecking order, a kind of artistic chain of command, and if you get a sense that an individual may not have the underlying strength and humility to truly assist you, do not ask for his help.

The fourth and last quality I look for in a helper is creativity, in hopes that he will be able to make some great suggestions as the show develops during rehearsals. But notice that the other three qualities matter more, at least to me. Lord knows I can always use some fresh creative imput, but not from an assistant who is not at least as positive, responsive, and emotionally secure as he is creative.

Assistants can be hazardous in another way as well. In my experience there have been times, especially during rehearsals and just before actual performances, when I have been tempted to indulge in what I call "flights from self"—chatting or horsing around with an assistant when I really should have been focusing my thoughts and feelings. In such moments, I suspect I am actually trying to *avoid myself,* probably out of nerves. Part of me believes that a "break" from self-awareness is as valuable as a brief vacation, a stress release; when you later refocus, your energy is often renewed and you approach the task at hand with fresh eyes. On the other hand, there have been times where my fatigue or nerves got the best of me and I found myself seeking distraction to the detriment of the rehearsal or show.

Be aware of this possible unconsious temptation and keep in mind that, as important as it it to take breaks, it is at least as important to develop your ability to *concentrate,* to stay in "one place" for an extended period of time so that you can thoroughly delve into a scene, action, phrase, or any other aspect of the monologue process. I have even heard it said that perhaps none of us is any "smarter" or more "intelligent" than anyone else. Some of us are simply better at concentrating our attention.

Is it okay to take a glass of water with me onstage?

By all means. I myself never take stage, any stage, without a glass of water. And I don't like the water to be too cold, because that usually invites condensation to build up on the glass. In my eyes a glass of water is not only lovely to look at and keeps your whistle wet, but it can be a wonderful prop capable of a hundred and one imaginative uses.

As the audience filed into the theater for *Contents under Pressure,* they saw onstage an unusually large, clear plastic drinking glass, filled with water, sitting on a white wooden chair. I had drilled a few large holes in the seat of the chair and beneath the chair placed a large flashlight, switched on and pointing straight up. This not only clouded the chair in diffuse lighting, but filled the glass of water with light as well. It was a really nice (and inexpensive!) visual effect, and more importantly, given that *Contents* begins with a childhood recollection involving water, the visual was also relevant.

However, if you are planning to have a refreshment onstage, stick to water. Juice and soda both have too much potential to coat your tongue, upset your stomach, and (frankly) give you gas. Talk about contents under pressure! (Rim shot.) "Folks! I'll be here all this week, try the veal!"

Should I wear makeup?

> The audience will accept anything they are not given reason to disbelieve.
>
> —David Mamet

If you are playing a character other than yourself, makeup may well be essential, to look older, younger, hairier, and so on. But if you are playing "just yourself," some monologuists feel that makeup is unnecessary, especially when performing in a particularly intimate or informal setting. However, given that a monologue is first and foremost about *communication,* and effectively applied makeup serves to clarify and emphasize your facial expressions (particularly to those sitting near the back of the room), it only makes sense to use it.

Makeup can take the distracting shine off a forehead, make the eyebrows more distinctive, make the mouth more expressive. Again, if you either do not want to or do not feel comfortable wearing makeup, don't worry about it. It won't make or break your performance. But, remember what Mies van der Rohe said: "God is in the details."

Is there really more than one way to skin a cat?

Of course. Just don't let your neighbors see you doing it.

What should I wear onstage?

Our body is precious. It is our vehicle for awakening. Treat it with care.
—Achaan Chaa

Clothes are almost always a good idea. Then again, it depends on the nature of your monologue. For example, if your monologue is about unusual sexual practices, walking onstage wearing nothing but a six-foot string of breakfast sausages might be quite relevant. But it would be wise to keep in mind a few general clothing rules of theater. A white shirt or blouse usually is avoided because it tends to wash out your face. And if you sweat a lot, you may want to avoid a dark blue or black shirt because sweat stains can be extremely distracting.

It is also very important to wear clothing that makes you stand out from your background. After all, if people are going to watch you for more than even just a few minutes, you want to make it as easy for them as possible. So if you're performing in front of a green curtain, don't wear a green shirt (whatever the shade). I personally prefer to wear solid nonprimary colors, but then there are performers like Spalding Gray who seem to have a penchant for quiet plaids.

Above all else, your clothes should be comfortable. If your monologue is about the joys of beekeeping, it would of course make a great deal of sense to wear a beekeeper's outfit (complete with the netted hood). But considering how hot and uncomfortable this would be, it probably would be a big mistake. Only when you wear truly comfortable clothes will your body feel encouraged to be its most expressive and your mind its most focused. But if you can wear something that is both comfortable and interesting (and relevant!), then by all means do so.

What about wearing a hat, mask, or sunglasses?

It's been said that the "eyes are the mirror of the soul," and for good reason. It's amazing how, even from two hundred feet away, we can "read" an actor with an uncovered face better than one whose face is even partially covered. Yet it is no coincidence that many younger performers (and lawyers) are drawn to wearing hats, sunglasses, and masks. Revealing yourself can be frightening—but in the theater, there is no other way. So though sunglasses or masks may well suit a certain section of your monologue, I suggest you try to make it work without such unconscious shields, as tempting as they sometimes are. In fact, many actors take this idea of showing as much of their "true face" as possible so much to heart that they keep even their hair cut short or at least always keep longer hair tied back.

WHY IS THE POPE'S HAT SO DAMN TALL?

Answers to this important question have been bandied about for years. Some believe that the pope may in fact be a secret snacker and so keeps several pounds of fudge, marshmallows, and peanut brittle on his person at all times. Hence the hat—really just a "7-Eleven à tête." Other theorists maintain that the tall hat is nothing more than a vain attempt always to remain the center of attention even in a large crowd of people.

Then there are those passionate few who insist that inside that hallowed head covering there lies a Marilyn Monroe poster (the one with her standing on the outdoor air vent) along with one of those stock market ticker-tape machines. But perhaps the most likely explanation is that His Holiness has a thing for cowboys, and his towering headgear is the closest his faith allows him to wearing a white ten-gallon hat.

What if I sweat a lot onstage?

Your face is the page upon which the play is written.

—Unknown

I'm a bit of a sweater myself, so I understand what a concern this can be. To my mind, sweating profusely, apart from being annoying and distracting for the performer, can negatively influence your monologue in at least two other ways. First, it can send a message of "the performer is nervous" to the audience. And whether or not this is true, it is still not something you want an audience thinking. Second, a sweaty forehead can pull all-important focus from your face to the shine on your head.

But there are a few ways you can combat this insidious foe. For starters, drink lots of water, both before and during your monologue. Many people find that this will encourage your body's natural coolant system to take it easy, and so produce less sweat. Also be sure you are wearing the lightest, coolest clothes possible. And make sure the air onstage under those hot, bright lights is as well circulated as possible. Alas, not all small theaters have air conditioning, but in such cases you easily can rent a few small fans and have them quietly whirring in the wings.

Pancake makeup also can help. Expertly applied, it can not only soak up sweat, but keep the shine off your face. Personally, I am not averse to occasionally patting my face

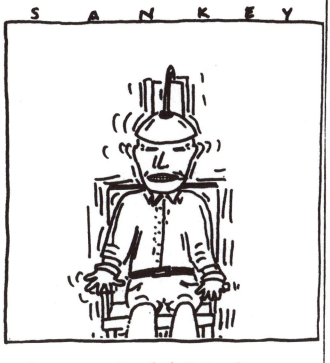

A MAN WITH THE HICCUPS
FRYING IN THE ELECTRIC CHAIR
DURING AN EARTHQUAKE

with a neatly folded handkerchief either, though I'd hesitate to combine the makeup with the handkerchief. It could make for quite a mess. And if all else fails, you may actually have to consider keeping your movements onstage to a minimum. But there is some good news. Sweating profusely is almost always at least partly a sign of nerves. So over time, as you become more comfortable and confident onstage, you will sweat less.

Are restaurant mints fattening?

No, but they should be avoided anyway. You see, studies have shown that the vast majority of the mints you find in bowls near the cash registers at restaurants are virtually covered with traces of human urine. This is because many people use the facilities in the restaurant, neglect to wash their hands, and then grab a handful of mints on the way out the door. Which is precisely why I always make a point of getting my mints on the way *in*.

Should I wear a watch onstage?

> *I am in the present. I cannot know what tomorrow will bring forth. I can know only what the truth is for me today. That is what I am called upon to serve, and I serve it in all lucidity.*
>
> —Igor Stravinsky

Some say wearing a watch onstage is the responsible thing to do because it allows you to keep an eye on the time in such situations as festivals, where you often have a venue for only an hour. Sixty minutes, not sixty-three. Others say that wearing a watch onstage is bad form, since it implicitly expresses a commitment to something other than "the moment." Whether this commitment unconsciously influences the audience members who notice the watch or merely influences the performer wearing it, so goes one argument, the watch is still an unwelcome presence in the theater. I'm torn on this issue and believe both sides have a definite point. But this much I do suggest: if you're going to wear a watch, don't get caught glancing at it. What a turnoff for the audience! Instead, incorporate such a glance into your physical actions—reaching for a glass of water, wiping your nose, petting a chicken—so that it goes completely unnoticed.

The Rehearsal

IS IT TRUE THAT, TO QUOTE MUHAMMAD ALI, "YOU CAN RUN BUT YOU CANNOT HIDE"?

Not quite. As we all fully realize, it is possible to both run and hide, sometimes even at the same time. But they are both temporary states. You certainly cannot run and/or hide forever and even to stay hidden for a considerable length of time, say a few weeks, is quite a feat, especially in this day of electronic surveillance equipment. However, if you insist on hiding, my only advice would be to hide behind something larger than yourself. For example, do not try to hide behind a midget. As charming as they can sometimes be, they are simply too small to hide behind. Mind you, if you could get your hands on say, three or four trustworthy, decent-sized midgets and you had them lock arms and stand in a row, well, then you might not be discovered for several days. Something to keep in mind.

Then again, if you yourself are a midget, perhaps you could indeed hide behind yet another midget. Though in such a case I would think you might have at least as much success with the old "I'm standing in front of a mirror" gag.

How should I rehearse?

Though we often live consciously on "automatic pilot," every one of us can learn to be awake. It just takes practice.

—Thich Nhat Hanh

Rehearse slowly and consciously. Do not race through your script and your stage blocking (where and how you will move onstage) and call it a day. Certainly there are times, later in your rehearsal process, when something is to be gained by "speed delivery" exercises. Such exercises can reinforce your memorization of the text, loosen up your delivery, and even allow you an opportunity to further explore your feelings about this or that section of your monologue. But these exercises should be saved for later.

When you are just starting, sit in a chair and slowly, mindfully, read your script aloud. Consume it with care and attention, like a fine meal, if only because anything you gloss over in the beginning will be only that much harder to access (both emotionally and intellectually) later on. Then after many such gentle read-throughs, stand up, put the chair in a corner, and as you deliver your text, begin to think and feel about how you may want to block it. Remember, performing is about *action*. But the most effective actors do nothing without a clear reason. They don't speak, they don't move, they don't even look—without a reason. By that I mean that even if the audience does not have a conscious sense of why you are saying or doing something, it is essential that you do. Effective blocking is *meaningful* blocking. It's not just a matter of standing there, walking over here, spending a few moments sitting down in the chair, and then getting up and standing again. Keep asking yourself, Why?

For example, you start your monologue sitting down, but at one point you decide to stand up. Why? Are you so excited that at that point, in the middle of some tale, you are suddenly moved to stand up and use your entire body to express yourself? If so, fine. That makes sense. If the audience feels that it is credible, they will not lose their focus. Actually, they are much more apt to increase their focus (always a blessing!). As you finish that brief story, you decide to take a few steps to the right. Why? Did you see some gum stuck to the floor of the stage, and you want to go and investigate? Fine, that makes sense (so long as you let the audience in on it somehow). Or maybe you want to silently increase the connection with the audience members to your right and deliver the next few lines of your script to them in particular, almost as if you just spotted an especially attentive face. Again, fine. That makes sense.

Once you have blocked out your stage movements and have the script firmly held in your heart and mind, now is the time you may want to think about such things as lighting and sound. Then again, some performers work the other way around, having a very particular vision of what lights and sounds they want and only then blocking out their movements accordingly. Either way, by now you are ready for full dress rehearsals. I suggest you do a lot of them. When you finally walk on that stage or into that space of sacred focus in front of an audience to give that very first real performance, you must be completely comfortable and familiar with the space.

You also should be timing your monologue as soon as possible. Nothing is more heartbreaking for a performer than spending a few weeks rehearsing a script, only to realize it's ten minutes too long! Timing your performance is much tougher than it sounds, especially if it has some sections that are funny (at least in theory!). Some audiences will laugh long and hard, others will barely chuckle. And all this dramatically affects the length of the performance. If you're renting a private space, five minutes one way or the other is no big deal. But if your performance is part of a larger program, you have the space for a maximum of one hour, and your monologue is "around" fifty-five minutes, five minutes can make all the difference in the world. In such a case, my advice is this: don't cut it close! It's not fair to the audience (who will be thinking about getting to another show two blocks away), it's not fair to the next

CLOWN FUNERAL

company that has to perform after you, and it's also not fair to yourself. Believe me, you will be under enough pressure.

One last suggestion about rehearsing. It's not a bad idea to have a few trusted friends sit in on an early rehearsal. Not so much to laugh at the funny parts, but just to witness what you are thinking of doing. Hand them each a piece of paper and a pen, sit them in a corner, and do your entire piece from start to finish (no stopping!). Encourage them to make notes when they feel like it, and then ask them for their thoughts at the end. Instead of discussing or (heaven forbid!) arguing any of their points, strive only to *hear them.* Tell your ego to go for a walk and come back in an hour. Spend a day or two thinking about what your friends said, and only then decide whether or not you are going to be influenced by any of their comments.

And speaking of making notes, it's also always a good idea to keep your own notepad nearby as you walk through a rehearsal. I find that those are the times when wonderful ideas about blocking, delivery, monologue order, and some last-minute script additions often make themselves known.

WHEN THE POLICE TELL US THAT SOMEONE WAS KILLED BECAUSE HE "FELL ASLEEP BEHIND THE WHEEL OF HIS CAR," HOW CAN THE POLICE KNOW THIS FOR SURE?

They can't. After all, in such instances the police simply find the wrecked car and the dead driver, nothing more. It's not as if they commonly find the driver dead in his car, wearing pajamas. Or find in the glove compartment an alarm clock that has yet to go off. Or even drool on the steering wheel.

What can I do to help me remember my lines?

The archer and his target are no longer separate objects, but are one reality. The archer ceases to be conscious of himself as the one who is engaged in hitting the bull's-eye which confronts him.

—Daisetz Suzuki

Learning lines is a very common concern, especially for inexperienced performers. Over time you will develop your own personal techniques for memorization, but I will tell you what I do. I start by reading the script over and over again, going "off book"—stopping and speaking a chunk from memory—as frequently as possible. Then I go back over, note what I may have missed, and jot down a word or two to remind me of it. You'll find that even by just taking such notes and writing down a few words, you will begin to remember the missed sentences.

Actually, don't think of them so much as a string of sentences as a *string of ideas*. Yes, you worked very hard to find the clearest, most concise words to express an idea, and you certainly should strive to use those words, but to "catch up" on a word or two during a live show at the price of the entire flow of your monologue is a serious error. In performance, I adhere closely to the lines that begin and end sections, but in the middle of these same sections I strive to stay open to inspiration, adding spontaneous lines as they occur to me. Ultimately, it's probably about a 90/10 split: 90 percent of the time I'm uttering lines right out of my written script, and 10 percent of the time I'm fleshing out certain thoughts, feelings, or experiences with improvised words and actions.

After a couple of weeks of memory work, you may still have a short list of ideas or sections you have yet to memorize completely. So spend some time working on just those sections. Don't waste your time trying to memorize stuff you have already memorized! Another worthwhile technique is to sit silently in a chair and, in your mind, quickly skim over the entire text of your monologue. Jump from the first sentence of a section to the last sentence of that section, and then to the first sentence of the next section and so on. It is particularly important that you feel comfortable and confident with these first and last lines (called "transitional concepts") to avoid ever feeling totally lost onstage.

But never become a slave to your text—no matter how well written! As hard as you worked on it, remember that it is but a tool, a *means* to convey a series of ideas, serving both as fuel and inspiration for your performance. It is not an end in itself. All should serve the final performance.

ARE DENTISTS HAPPY PEOPLE?

Statistically no. Believe it or not, dentists have an unusually high suicide rate. One explanation for this is that their patients are never truly happy to see them. Dentists spend most of their days causing people obvious pain and discomfort. After a while it starts to eat away at many dentists' spirits. So in a state of perpetual depression and perhaps even unconscious self-loathing, they take their own lives. But I say, instead of killing themselves, why don't they just . . . *stop hurting us?* Put down those sharp, pointy instruments, put away your high-speed drill, and come over here and give me a long, warm hug.

Should I direct myself or have someone else direct me?

Everything in the universe is connected, everything is osmosis. Inter-dependence rules the cosmic order.

—Taisen Deshimaru

I have worked with directors on a number of projects, but I have yet to have someone other than myself direct one of my live monologues. And I must admit, in retrospect I believe this has been a mistake. Certainly there is much to be said for trying to bring your own personal vision to the stage in as complete and detailed a form as possible. But as the performer and (often) writer, a monologuist already is bringing so much creative perspective to the project, the show will usually only benefit from the inspired input of others, especially those with theatrical experience. A good director brings to a production not only a second set of eyes and ears but a world of ideas and interpretations. And an effective monologue is much more than an instance of creative *expression*; it is also an instance of *communication*. In other words, as a monologuist your goal is not only to express yourself but to be seen, heard, and understood by your audience, and I believe it is in this matter of communication (rather than that of expression) that a director's imput can be invaluable.

But make no mistake. I do not think you should look to your director to supply ideas for scenes, moments, and transitions where you have none. As a monologuist, a director's ideas should be *in addition* to your own. This is why I suggest that if you decide to work with a director, be sure to arrive at your first meeting brimming with your own ideas and approaches. Of course, some of these will be inspired and some less so, but together you and your director can sort through them as the director also adds his or her own ideas.

And above all else, *listen to your director!* Whenever working with others, I always try to work with the best people I can and then let them do their job. Yes, it can be a little unnerving trusting others past a certain point, especially when it comes to creative matters, and especially considering that as a monologuist you will be the only one onstage "living or dying" as you follow their advice. But before you

THE GLIB REAPER

even consider working with other people in the theater, whether they are directors, makeup artists, or set designers, be sure to ask yourself, Am I truly open to including their ideas in my vision? If not, do everyone a big favor and try to do it all yourself. Not only will you avoid wasting other people's precious time, but you will also at least be able to focus upon your own creativity, without having to deceive other people (or yourself) about the degree to which you are sincerely receptive to their input.

SIX PERCENT OF THE HUMAN POPULATION IS BORN WITH AN EXTRA FINGER. IS THIS A GOOD THING?

Well, I remember back in grade four there was this girl Lila who had a sixth finger. Sort of an extra little . . . niblet, I guess you could call it. It looked pretty strange, but she *was* the school "scissors, paper, rock" champ. Whenever Lila played, it was like she whipped out some kind of organic Swiss Army knife. Scissors, paper, rock, corkscrew . . . you never knew what was going to come up. Like most of the kids, I lost a lot of money that year. But I learned a few things, too. Like, Don't play games with mutants if there's big money involved. Stuff like that.

The Audience

Who should I invite to my first performance?

The audience will teach you how to act and the audience will teach you how to write and to direct.

—David Mamet

Approach your first performance as if it is a dress rehearsal. Actually, considering that the audience is an integral part of any effective performance, your first live performance is really the first time the entire "cast" is assembled. In this sense, you and your audience are partners in the same production. Your first live performance is the time to begin to get a sense of how to, if not include, at least *respond to* the audience's subtle reactions to your work. Listen and feel carefully, and an audience will change your work for the better. But though you certainly would like as many people at your premiere as possible, you probably don't want critics or other important decision makers present for this first attempt.

Who then? Well, to such performances many actors invite friends and family, people they can count on to be positive and supportive. But some monologists (like myself) prefer to try out their monologues on complete strangers, people who will give an utterly immediate and honest audience response to every moment of a monologue. As for my family and friends, before inviting them I prefer to have first performed the piece for at least a few guinea pig audiences. What can I say? I'd like my family and friends to see my creative work at its best.

What if nobody comes to my performance?

Flow with whatever may happen and let your mind be free. Stay centered by accepting whatever you are doing. This is the ultimate.
—Chang-tzu

An empty house can be a marvelous test of emotional management. And believe me, I *know*. I still can remember a night, many years ago, when one person showed up for one of my performances. One soul. And no, it wasn't a friend. And to be completely honest, I must admit (with cheeks still a little flushed), back then I just didn't have the guts to "go on with the show." Previous to the show, I had broken one of the cardinal rules of show business: I had amassed a mountain of expectations. And such a mountain tends to take on a life of its own, transforming mere expectations into heartfelt *needs*.

So there I was, a few minutes before the curtain was supposed to go up (granted, the curtain was little more than a blanket hung in front of a drab matchbox of a stage). When I saw that despite all the hard work I had done trying to promote the show, only one single person had shown up, I was not only crushed but felt I didn't have what I needed to go on with the show. Looking back, I feel it was definitely bad form, if only because such an attitude failed to honor one person's sincere interest in what I had to say. But that night I just didn't have the emotional resources. So I quickly ran outside to a nearby convenience store, bought a chocolate bar, rushed back into the theater "space," handed my only patron his money back along with the chocolate bar, and mumbled an apology as I stared in shame at the floor. I then literally ran out the back door of the club. Mortified, heart-broken, and with tears streaming down my face, I ran for several blocks through the unusually dark night. (What can I say? I'm a pretty sensitive guy.)

Don't do what I did. If only one person—or even nobody!—is gracious enough to turn up for one of your per-formances, I strongly advise you to bloody well perform! You rented (or at least prepared) the space, so go ahead and make the most of it. Think of it as a dress rehearsal. The

HOME COOKING

odds are extremely good that you can benefit from yet another. And you may want to bear in mind the words of someone I once heard on the radio (I didn't catch his name, but his voice has been with me ever since): "I was quite lucky not to become successful until later in life."

How can I keep the audience interested?

Learn your lines and don't trip over the furniture.
—Spencer Tracy, advice to young actors

Two words are the key to keeping an audience's attention: *information* and *emotion.* In other words, share your thoughts and feelings—the more detailed, intimate, and honest, the better. Be truthful and be passionate.

WHICH COUNTRY IN THE WORLD HAS THE HIGHEST NUMBER OF SCHIZOPHRENICS PER CAPITA?

Russia. Look it up, it's true. So who knows . . . we're always hearing about long lines for food, but maybe it's really just a couple of people. Mind you, this unusually high percentage of schizophrenics at least explains the Russian people's obsession with those Russian Doll sets. A little person inside another person, inside another person! Crazy, baby.

What if the audience gets bored or tired?

Well, then, you are doing something wrong. Unfortunately, attention spans aren't what they used to be. Can you believe that a hundred years ago entire families would routinely sit on hard wooden benches in churches listening to everything from sermons to organized debates for as long as four or five hours? Today our attention spans are so short, we actually have a name for a malady that seems to be on the increase: ADD, "attention deficit disorder." Many people seem to require the promise of computer-generated fireworks to find the patience to sit still in a plush seat for even ninety minutes.

I'm not saying you have to have a lot of song and dance in your monologue, just that you always should keep in mind the attention span of your audience. Certainly stay true to the spirit of your monologue and what it is you want to communicate. But try to do so in the most engaging and interesting manner possible. To communicate rather than merely express, you very much need an audience's avid attention *and* emotional involvement.

Stay interesting, stay stimulating. If you're a relatively inexperienced performer, it may well be a better idea to vary the subject matter (the "topics") of your monologue rather than try to do an in-depth exploration of a single theme. Though admirable, a single-minded performance is much harder to sell than one where the performer moves on to a fresh topic every few minutes.

But there is something else to consider if and when you ever sense that an audience is bored or tired. For if you notice that the audience is bored, you as a performer must first have already disconnected from the focus of your performance. That very disconnection can only serve to heighten the audience's own lack of emotional involvement. Remember, as tempting as it sometimes is to pull your focus away from the script in an attempt to connect with your audience, it is only by *maintaining your focus* on the script that you will reconnect with the audience. Paradoxically, it is often when you are least aware of the audience that you are most intimately connected with them.

If you sense the audience is becoming restless, chances are you too are becoming restless. Who became unfocused first? You or them? It really doesn't matter. What matters is that you and your audience are intimately tied, and it is up to you somehow to rediscover your focus as soon as possible. Performing is exhausting work, both physically and emotionally, and being able to reestablish your focus and rhythm is essential. For just as rhythm can work for you, it also can work against you. Think of a drummer beating out a perfectly steady rhythm, but not in time with the rest of the band! In a sense, the drummer's rhythm is perfectly wrong—perfect, *but* wrong.

In performance you can establish a rhythm that is constantly connecting you with your material, your energy, and your audience, just as you can establish a rhythm that, as steady as it is, keeps you out of sync with the same things. If you feel you are caught up in this kind of destructive rhythm, you must do everything within your power to break it—immediately. This can be as simple as taking a few short breaths or taking a moment to notice something at the back of the theater.

If this isn't working, you might have to do something a little more extreme. You might, for example, jump ahead in your script a few paragraphs to a favorite section you always look forward to sinking your teeth into. You may even want to consider asking someone in the audience a question pertaining to what you were just talking about. This last option is particularly daring and can not only jar an audience but also kill any established rhythm. Alternatively, done in the right way, some audiences will find this break from script utterly charming. And anyway, if the previous rhythm wasn't working, perhaps anything is better.

WHY DO THEY FIRE RIFLES AT A MILITARY FUNERAL?

I'm not sure, but I think it's quite rude. After all, the major-ity of soldiers that die have been shot to death. So I cannot think of anything more insensitive than firing off a couple of rounds over the coffin in front of grief-stricken family and friends. What's next? Waving an automobile tire over the grave of people killed in hit-and-runs? Or what about clang-ing large axes over the grave of anyone chopped to pieces by a deranged serial killer? Whatever happened to funerals being silent, somber affairs? With our culture's irreverent, even flippant attitude toward death, it's just a matter of

A BRUSH WITH DEATH

time until the names of funeral homes undergo a change as well. Instead of Johnson & Hargrave, Funeral Directors, we're going to start seeing names like Steve's Bone Palace. I can just imagine the clown standing outside on the sidewalk holding black balloons. Oh well. I guess that's progress for you.

What if the audience laughs at the wrong places?

Learn to respond, not react.

—Angarika Sujata

There are no "wrong places" for an audience to laugh, just places you, the writer/performer, did not plan or expect them to laugh. Of course, if such laughter harms the tone, spirit, or pacing of that part of your monologue, you probably will want to consider cutting, rewriting, or at least rearranging the material. Even a simple shift in your delivery might do the trick. Then again, laughter is such a wonderful thing, I suggest you first try to figure out a way to keep the "unplanned funny part" and work *with* it, not *against* it. (Another very Zen outlook.)

What if the audience doesn't laugh at the funny parts?

Well, then, blame the audience. I'm kidding! And yet many disappointed performers do just that. And it drives me nuts. How ridiculous! Think about it—the audience not only shows up in good faith, but often even pays to listen to us for close to an hour, sitting on hard seats, giving us their full attention. But if they seem less than enthralled for even a moment, some performers actually will blame the audience rather than themselves. How mortal, how sad.

I know it doesn't feel good to stand up in front of people, try your best, and get the definite sense that the audience is unmoved and unimpressed. But instead of blaming them (or ourselves, for that matter), I think we all would be better served if we simply thank them for coming to see us and do what we can to learn from their responses and reactions. So if the audience doesn't laugh at your "hilarious" story about the first time your aunt took you to a massage parlor...well then, perhaps it just isn't especially funny. No great loss.

One of the classic questions artists must ask themselves is, Should I invest my time refining my more obvious strengths or developing my weaker sides? Or both? There's no easy answer, especially given that there is much to be gained by taking either or both roads. Though what is gained by taking this or that road will be different from what is gained by taking the others. So again, the question comes down to, As a performer and writer, what exactly do I hope to achieve? If you can't always exploit your strengths consistently, at least be aware of them.

WHY ARE BABIES SO COMPLETELY USELESS?

Frankly, this question is a bit cynical, but considering that it is the rare infant that can carry on a lively conversation about world politics, help you move a couch, or even make a decent cup of coffee, I guess it's also a fair question. And the answer is quite simple. Though tiny newborns are certainly sweet and dear, their true value lies not so much in what they are today as in what they will *become*. Today they may be only tiny, gurgling, self-centered dependents, but give them even just a few years and they typically become small, nimble humans capable of any number of household duties—really nothing more than pink-faced slaves eager to wash windows or even make toast so long as they believe your love for them hangs in the balance. But bless their hearts, they grow up quickly, so make the most of it while you can.

What if I hear people talking during my monologue?

Water is stronger than rock.

—Zen koan

This is extremely rare, but unfortunately it does happen, especially in less formal performance settings. In such situations you usually can count on someone in the audience to shush the offending individuals, but if after a minute or two nobody comes to your rescue, you have two options. Talk over them, or try to get them to shut up. Personally, I don't much like the first option. Oh, I've done it. Once. But in retrospect I think I let down the more attentive souls in the audience. They had a right to hear my monologue undisturbed, and though it would have been nice for someone in the audience to be the disciplinarian, the responsibility ultimately lies on my shoulders.

This leaves you with the second option of getting them to shut up. I've done this three or four times in a few different contexts, and I've always done it in the same way—not by directly engaging them (which can send a subtle signal of a lack of control to the rest of the audience) but by indirectly communicating to them through humor. All I did was take a single step in their direction and continue my monologue without missing a beat. Then I lifted my head ever so slightly and, without changing my volume or tone, continued to perform my monologue, but imagined I was delivering it directly to the chatters. The audience immediately picked up on this, laughed, and by the time the laugh died down, the reprobates invariably had stopped talking. Remember, go with the flow.

ARE PARROTS PSYCHIC?

Extremely. Biologists and animals experts have been wondering about this for years. Recent studies indicate that if someone standing within a few feet of a healthy, well-adjusted parrot merely *thinks* of a playing card, more often than not the parrot somehow knows which card the person has in mind. How is this possible? Nobody knows for sure, but this "mental link" seems most readily established between parrots and their primary caregivers. The army is of course working to develop an entire flock of parrots able to follow and read the minds of political leaders in far-off countries, but the difficulty is that precious few parrots speak more than one language.

7

The Performance

Do I have to be an actor?

Live every act fully, as if it were your last.

—Buddhist saying

You don't necessarily have to be an actor, but you definitely should be passionately interested in *performing*. Obviously it can only help your performance if you are a professionally trained actor, but if you are not, chances are it is still well within your grasp to intrigue, delight, and entertain an audience as long as you are interested in both practicing and performing. And by "performing" I mean nothing less than a passionate desire to bring your script *to life!* It will require much rehearsal, commitment, and daring, but I have no doubt that if you are serious about your monologue, you will be able to rise to the challenge.

Many before you have done it, so why not you? I fully appreciate that getting onstage can be a terrifying idea for someone who is not an experienced performer, but rather than focusing on the reasons not to do it, focus on the reasons *to do it!*

Should I play a "character"?

The actor, in learning to be true and simple, in learning to speak to the point despite being frightened, and with no certainty of being understood, creates his own character; he forges character in himself.
—David Mamet

A character is really nothing more than a perspective or collection of sentiments that are at least slightly different from your own everyday perspective. A character is an *outlook* that is typically not yours. However, one of the reasons movie actors come to be typecast, playing very similar roles from one film to the next, is because they are able to relate strongly to that "type" of character. In other words, the character closely resembles at least one aspect of the actor's real experience or personality. In fact, this is precisely what often *makes* a character a character, namely that it is but a single aspect of a personality, theatrically exaggerated to dominate the entire person. In the film *The Silence of the Lambs,* Anthony Hopkins's character is that of a psychotic, emotionally detached, brilliant serial killer. I don't for a moment believe that in real life Hopkins is like that. I do, however, believe that some part of his real personality can at least relate to the *idea* of being emotionally cut off and of harboring monstrous, profound malice toward others.

A character, then, is essentially an exaggeration, however slight, but one that has as its seed a perspective to which you the performer can nonetheless relate. As for playing a character during your monologue, most monologuists do not strive to play a character. Instead, they work to be as much their own true selves as possible! No easy task, I assure you—especially onstage in front of two hundred strangers. But there are those monologuists who do adopt a definite character for their entire performance. This is perhaps most commonly done when one is performing a monologue about a famous historical personality such as Mark Twain or Vincent van Gogh. Though more often than not, one of the implicit challenges in the monologue form is that of being as real and as powerfully intimate as possible.

WHY ARE GIANTS AND SANTA CLAUS BOTH RENOWNED FOR SHOUTING "HO HO HO"?

It all springs from the fact that people seldom feel comfortable inviting mythical characters into their homes to spend the night. As a result, when traveling far from home, entities such as giants and Santa Claus are often without a place to rest their heads, and understandably they long to talk about it. But the pain is simply too great, their disappointment in humanity all-consuming. And so the closest they can come to breaching the subject is shouting the word *hotel*. But even this one word they have a hard time completing. Hence the "ho" sound. The typically desperate, almost stuttering repetition ("Ho . . . ho . . . ho . . .") only serves to further substantiate my theory.

Who would pay money to listen to me talk?

Actually, "talking" is not what a monologue is about. Rather, it is about *performing* in such a way that an audience is stimulated. And for that, people will pay money (sometimes quite a lot). Your goal should be not to talk or even merely "present," but to use your script and performance so that the audience undergoes a completely engaging experience.

How can I give a great performance?

Find your mark, look the other fellow in the eye, and tell the truth.
—James Cagney

Nobody can guarantee a truly great performance. After all, greatness is a truly mysterious thing. But I *can* give you a few tips about how you might be able to improve the chances of giving at least a "good" performance. First, strive to be honest, both with yourself and with your audience. If during rehearsals a line sounds "tinny," ringing false time

OLD PIPES

and again, cut it. Make the most of such an editing privilege. Believe me, it's rare for a performer. In my attempt to establish a truthful relationship with audiences, I sometimes think about an expression I've heard in both writing and performing circles, "from the heart to the heart." In other words, that which is spoken or shared from the heart of one person is most apt to move the heart of another.

Second, trust your script. If (as I hope) you have slaved over your script for weeks, if not months, trust the amount of effort you put into it. Don't betray all that sweat and loving attention by lacking the courage to speak your lines with everything you have. And third, rehearse. Rehearse, rehearse, rehearse! It's a cliché, but that makes it no less true: you must rehearse your lines so well that, in effect, you forget them. Only then will you be able to invest all your energy in the moment, up on that stage performing. Really *performing*.

How can I get the audience to like me?

Learn to let go. That is the key to happiness.

—Achaan Chaa

I don't think you can "get" an audience to like you. You can only be your most effective, honest, and engaging self . . . and hope for the best. However, it wouldn't hurt to remember that two of the most important qualities of any live performance are *likability* and *vulnerability*. Even if you are playing a mean or unkind character, there still has to be something likable about the character. If an audience does not, in some sense, like you as a person onstage, they cannot feel both with you and for you. Without that investment, all theatrical efforts will fail.

An audience must also feel that you are really there, onstage, *for them,* and not merely rattling off a script in your head or going through the motions of your performance. They should have a sense that nothing stands between you and them—no fear, no script, no distracting thoughts or intentions. Just you and them. The monologue form is built on a seemingly spontaneous sharing, and on a powerful sense of intimacy. Be there, really there onstage for them, and they will be there for you.

What should I do just before I go onstage?

Imagine that the air you are breathing is fog and visualize it coming through your nose and throat into the abdomen. Let it circulate there and through your body and your limbs. "

—Joe Hyams

Breathing exercises are the perfect thing to do before going onstage. With even a little practice you will find that such exercises relax and refresh the body while also calming the mind. And visualization (as in the above example) prevents your mind from gravitating toward fearful or anxious thoughts. Of course you fervently want to delight the audience, to be stirring and fascinating. But I think it's better to focus upon your desire simply to communicate. Be true to your script. Be honest with your audience. Meditating is also a fine thing to do. I provide a description of a "sitting meditation" at the back of the book.

Just before you walk onstage, it also can be a good idea to remember how hard you have worked to get there and what you hope to accomplish during your performance. But, don't psych yourself out by putting undue pressure on yourself. Yes, you've worked hard, and yes, you would like the audience to like you, but don't let your often anxious musings result in a stressful focus on power (them vs. you vs. them).

Just as the audience's experience matters, so does yours. Winning the audience's approval is a real tightrope walk. Care—but not too much. And remember, you will probably never see any of these people again! You're not out merely to give, but to receive as well. Perform for them, but also for yourself and for your own growth as an artist and an evolving creature. Maintaining this balance is one of theater's greatest challenges.

I'm feeling a little nervous. How about having a couple of beers before going onstage?

This is always a good idea. Better yet, drop acid or maybe smoke a little crack, just to clear your thoughts and as a pick-me-up. I'm kidding, of course. I would strongly advise anyone interested in a *long-term* creative career (even if it's just a hobby) to avoid the use of any kind of drugs, alcohol, or ritualistic behavior in connection with their art. I cannot say it is always easy for any of us to get in touch with our creative voice, but to involve a substance or routine that lies outside ourselves is only to set ourselves up for eventual disaster.

I once knew of a writer who felt that he had to move to another city whenever beginning a new book. Not only did this get rather expensive, but it didn't always work. So there he was, far from family and friends, with not even his art to comfort him or give his days meaning. In my experience, performance demands patient, studious reflection and backbreaking work. Nothing else helps. Of course, history suggests that there have been those complex souls who are able to produce brilliant work under the influence of a variety of stimulants. But I would wager that for every "successful" artist who is able to produce quality work from the bottom of a bottle there are thousands who try and fail. Do you really want to try to beat odds like that?

Work hard and have the courage to step onstage in front of all those people—sober. Believe me, you'll get much more out of it that way.

How should I walk onstage?

If you walk, just walk. If you sit, just sit; but whatever you do, don't wobble.

—Ummon

You should take the stage relaxed, focused, energized, and filled with a strong desire to share. With a nod of your head or just a look in your eye, acknowledge and even welcome the audience to "your theater." It is, after all, *yours* (at least for the next fifty minutes or so). It is your home, your church, your domain. You are the host and the audience, your guests. I suggest you keep that very much in mind.

Classic acting theory suggests that as you step on that stage, you should send "invisible threads of positive energy" from your eyes toward the audience, and not just to the people in the front row. In fact, it's usually better to send your energy to the back row, in that way "binding" the audience to one another and you to the audience. Then, in humility and confidence . . . utter the first words of your script. Begin.

How should I begin my monologue?

We carry with us the wonders we seek without us.
—Sir Thomas Browne

During their first few moments onstage, many monologuists attempt to establish a sense of time and place: "When I was seventeen I spent three months traveling through Germany and Italy...." Or, "I love sitting on the roof of my apartment building at night staring up at the moon...." The goal of your first few moments is to forge as many different links with the audience as possible, emotional, conceptual, narrative, and so on. Bear in mind that no matter how engaging a performer may be, during the first minute of almost any monologue the audience is still settling in. Even though they may be consciously focused on you and your words, on an unconscious level they are actively assessing and integrating a million and one details about the performance space, your attire, the lighting, the seat they are sitting in, and so forth. So though on one hand you would like your first few moments onstage to be as powerful as possible, realize that most audiences nonetheless will take at least a few minutes to get on your bus.

How should I deliver my monologue?

Delivery is the tone, pitch, and rhythm with which you speak your lines, and though your delivery will vary depending on the script, the performance, the audience, and the venue, there are still some general performance guidelines to consider, especially as a monologuist.

For example, it's usually a good idea to speak to the crowd as if they were a single person across a coffee table from you, but beware talking to just a single member of the audience or even merely the front two rows. Also, never forget that the audience is forever looking to you to see *how they should feel* about what you say. They hear your words and see your actions, but there are still a great many ways to interpret the underlying meaning of what you are sharing with them. And though a line of script undoubtedly will mean different things to different people, the audience is still very interested in (even in need of) understanding what your words mean *to you.*

Don't leave them guessing. Share. Do you feel sad? Elated? Worried? Excited? Resigned? I'm reminded of a lyric from a song by Crowded House, "Everywhere you go, you take the weather with you." This is equally true onstage, especially for the monologuist. Your perceived mood has at least as much influence upon a theatrical moment as your words. Perhaps more.

Is it okay if I decide to deliver my monologue in a language other than English?

Again, it all depends. First, are you able to speak fluently in this other language? I find that it is always a good idea when getting up to talk in front of a group of people to be able to speak in the language I have chosen to employ. Otherwise, it just gets confusing for everyone. Also, it is extremely important that you always ask yourself, What language does the audience speak? If, for example, they speak English, delivering your monologue in German or Cantonese, though initially intriguing, will become tiresome after even just a few minutes.

During my monologue, what should I do when I want to stop talking about one subject and start talking about another?

When you are at sea, keep clear of the land.

—Publilius Syrus

This question of transitions is extremely important. In fact, both the audience's interest and the performer's focus is most commonly lost during transitions. When Spalding Gray has finished talking about a topic or has come to the end of one of his brief stories, he will sometimes take a moment to sip from his glass of water or flip a page in his notebook. He uses these practical devices to great effect, allowing the audience a few moments to absorb what he has just finished talking about before launching into something else.

And note that this "new topic" needn't always relate clearly to the previous subject. Just as our minds sometimes (seem to) jump from one unrelated subject to another, so too do many effective monologues. But again, not all monologuists have the same style. Many prefer instead to have definite "throughlines" running from one story or reflection to another. Such throughlines are commonly either topic-oriented or emotionally based. An example of a typical transition based on topic would be first to talk about spending two years in therapy, and then go on to talk about the effects of Prozac on a romantic relationship. An example of an emotionally based transition would be to talk about how much you loved your family dog and then begin talking about how much you love skiing. In the latter case, it is not so much what you are talking about, but rather how you *feel* about it.

What about pacing?

Time and space are fragments of the infinite for the use of finite crea-
tures.

—Henri Frederic Amiel

Pacing is the *rhythm* of your monologue, the tempo of your
speaking, moving, even your breathing. It's the rhythm of
your performance as you move from one subject to another,
from one sentence to another, and from one syllable to
another. And note that concern for the rhythm of such
things necessarily requires you not just to be aware of but
even to *control* the modulation, variety, and tempo of your
voice and movement.

There are probably as many different tempi as there are people, but undoubtedly some are more effective than others, especially when it comes to monologuing. What makes for an "effective" tempo or rhythm? Yet again, it comes down to such qualities as clarity, expressiveness, and engagement. The best monologuists trust their feelings more than their thoughts, particularly when it comes to tempo. As you write your monologue, try to vary your emotional terrain rather than spending too much time being "sad" or "excited" or "angry." Or if you want to spend an extended period of time exploring one emotion in particular, be sure to apply yourself to varying the *hues* of that emotion.

In essence, tempo is a kind of tightrope walk. Too much variety, and you surely will lose your audience; too little variety, and the monotony of your performance will dull the focus and interest of even the most forgiving of audiences.

What about pausing?

The quieter you become the more you can hear.
—Baba Ram Dass

Konstantin Stanislavsky teaches that there are two kinds of pauses in the theater: the first logical, the second psychological. Logical pauses are those you take between words, sentences, or actions, brief moments of silence aiding the listener to see, hear, and interpret whatever you happen to be doing or saying on stage. Such pauses are there primarily for clarity's sake.

Psychological pauses, however, are those silences which the performer "plants," "generates," and even "explores" for the sake of the pathos of the performance. They are not, strictly speaking, "necessary," but add an enormous amount to a performance when used with skill, intuition, and restraint. These are the pauses which appear as you search for a word or get lost in a thought. What, then, is the difference between the pause of an inexperienced performer trying to remember his line and the pause of a seasoned actor emphasizing a word she has just uttered? Control. Deliberation. Intentionality. All of which ultimately yield an essentially different feeling in the audience and performer alike.

What if I forget my lines?

This is the nightmare of all performers: drawing a blank onstage. Nothing else quite so quickly brings sweat to the brow and grinds a performance to an uncomfortable halt. My advice is, of course, to rehearse enough that you *know* your lines. But let's say that despite your best and most diligent efforts, you feel that there is still a real chance you might either forget a line, or worse, an entire section of your monologue. In that case, I strongly suggest you use a set list.

A set list is basically a single sheet of paper, maybe even just a file card, with a row of words written on it, each word standing for a section of your monologue. Such a list does at least three things. First, it helps you avoid missing a section entirely. Second, it helps you remember the overall order of your monologue. And third, *just knowing it is there* can be supremely reassuring. The list can be under your glass of water on a stool or taped to the back of a prop (I once had mine taped to the back of a suitcase) or even just lying by your feet on the stage.

Some performers actually take a notepad up onstage. Such monologuists don't so much read from it as occasionally flip through it between stories, recollections, or "rants" on various topics. But remember that frequent and obvious use of a notepad does, on some level, infringe upon the relationship between the performer and the audience.

INSTEAD OF TRYING TO KILL VAMPIRES WITH WOODEN STAKES AND SILVER BULLETS, WHY DON'T PEOPLE JUST DRIVE OVER THEM WITH REALLY BIG TRUCKS?

Well for starters, most vampires can fly. So unless you plan on driving these "really big trucks" up some kind of steep ramp and launching them high into the air in hopes of knocking the bloodsuckers flat on their asses, I don't think the trucks (big or otherwise) are going to work. Big trucks are also quite expensive, even just to rent for the night. And rental people tend to be very fussy about scratched doors and dented fenders. So I say, stick with the stakes and bullets. Unoriginal, but effective.

How should I end my monologue?

> There is no end. There is no beginning. There is only the infinite passion of life.
>
> —Federico Fellini

Psychologists use the ideas of "primacy" and "recency." These temporally oriented Siamese twins usually are found lumbering through the halls of behaviorist thinking. Primacy deals with our *first* impression of a thing or person, and recency deals with our *last* (or at least most recent). The point is that both impressions have their power and influence.

If pressed (as I often am), I would have to say that how you begin your monologue is more important than how you end it, if only because without an effective beginning, you will not have the audience's trust. And without that you are nowhere. However, your monologue's ending will not only be the audience's very last impression of your show (the one that they will take out into the street with them), it is also an ideal opportunity to bring various elements of your monologue to a culmination.

This is why many effective monologues end on a high note of some kind—a story, passage, song, or string of ideas that is especially funny, moving, tragic, ironic, insightful, or poetic. (Note the key word, *especially*.) And if, in addition, you can end your monologue in such a way that the ending somehow makes sense to the audience, all the better. Ideally, you want the ending of your monologue to be an experience that will resonate within the hearts and minds of the audience for hours, days, or even years afterward.

In *Contents under Pressure* I attempt to achieve this by bringing the audience back to one of my childhood memories (my earliest one, actually), with which I in fact *began* the monologue. I wrote it this way in the hope that the elliptical effect of ending where I began would give the audience a sense of gentle irony, while also suggesting that perhaps we each spend much of our lives struggling within the fierce grips of our earliest memories.

Should I take a bow at the end?

Not necessarily. It all depends on how you feel and what suits your personality and style (at least while onstage). But this much I do advise: In some way, almost in any way, gratefully acknowledge your audience. They just sat there listening to you, focused on you for a good chunk of time. They could have been watching a movie featuring millions of dollars of special effects or eating a nice meal or even catching up on some sleep at home.

But instead, they invested their precious time watching you and listening to you talk about some of your most intimate thoughts and feelings. I believe such a gift deserves to be acknowledged. A quick, short bow is fine, as is a heartfelt nod of the head, something that feels right and conveys respect and gratitude.

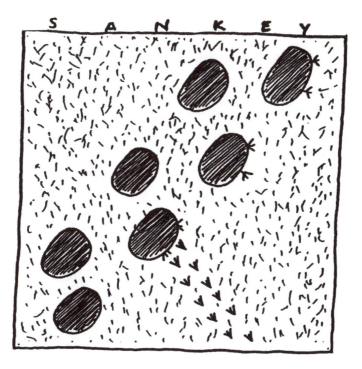

Chicken Meets Elephant

Is skiing really that dangerous?

Absolutely. I realize that it is considered to be one of the oldest and most revered sports in the world and that there are even ancient cave drawings depicting humans sliding down slopes with long pieces of wood tied to their feet, but how do we know what such a cave drawing really means? Back in primitive times, between hunting for food and staying warm, who had time to scribble on walls? Someone nursing a *broken leg,* that's who. Such drawings aren't an homage to the joys of skiing, but rather a warning: "Don't do this! You'll break your goddamn neck! I almost did!"

How can I become a more confident performer?

> *The swordmaster is as unself-conscious as the beginner. The nonchalance which he forfeited at the beginning of his instruction he wins back again at the end as an indestructible characteristic. But unlike the beginner, he holds himself in reserve, is quiet and unassuming, without the least desire to show off.*
> —Eugen Herrigel, *Zen in the Art of Archery*

Confidence comes from rehearsals, experience, and belief. Experience onstage itself in no way guarantees excellence or understanding. The old adage "Practice makes perfect" would perhaps be more accurately expressed as, "Only perfect practice makes perfect." There is no substitute for consciously applying yourself to the task of learning, wringing as much understanding and insight as you can from every moment you spend onstage. Actually, don't just "spend" time onstage—invest it! And one of the keys to such an investment is not only to prepare prior to going onstage, but also to review what happened onstage when you walk off-stage. Only then will true, trustworthy confidence come.

Less experienced performers mistake a loud voice and bold gestures for confidence. This is seldom the case. Confidence doesn't betray itself with a booming voice or desperate stage movements. Real confidence comes from a realistic belief in your abilities and in your right to stand in front of an audience and share your truth. As with applause, a performer's confidence is most often *earned*. In such matters, there are no shortcuts.

How can I keep my performances fresh?

Angels can fly because they take themselves lightly.
—G. K. Chesterton

If you are planning to perform your monologue only once, twice, or even just a handful of times, I suspect you will have very little problem giving fresh performances. This will be especially true if you are a relatively inexperienced monologuist. If, however, you are planning on performing a monologue more than eight or ten times, keeping it fresh can be a real challenge. One tip is to not *over*rehearse. As soon as you feel you have a good grasp on the material, cut back on your rehearsal schedule. When I begin rehearsing a monologue, it is not uncommon for me to "walk through it" three or even four times in a day. But when the dates of the actual performance draw closer, I make a point of rehearsing only once a day. You don't want to run out of steam or, to put it another way, dull the corners of your thoughts and (particularly) your feelings. Ideally, you want to take the stage for every performance filled with an air of discovery and curiosity.

Another technique you can use to combat predictability and boredom is to practice certain sections of your monologue in isolation rather than sandwiched between the usual other sections. However, you should only attempt this once you are confident you have memorized the entire order of your piece.

Why is "intimacy" so important onstage?

Onstage you are striving to achieve a seamless cohesion between various elements—between you and your script,

TAXIDERMIST WITH A SENSE OF HUMOR

resulting in a convincing performance, and between your performance and the audience, resulting in a powerful experience. Such an intimacy of connection is perhaps only attainable by means of a real, vulnerable, alive sharing. And thankfully, by its very nature the monologue form nurtures just such an intimacy between the script, the performer, the performance, and the audience.

DURING MY MONOLOGUE IS IT OKAY IF I CRY A LOT?

In performance, shared emotion is almost always more effective than shared thought. But if you find yourself crying even during the more lighthearted sections in your monologue (assuming there *are* some lighthearted sections!) you may want to seek professional help. Best of luck.

What does it mean to "stay visual"?

> *Art is a technique of communication. The image is the most complete technique of all communication.*
>
> —Claes Oldenburg

Theater is about action. And though speaking is certainly a type of action, it is not as immediate as doing something more overtly physical. Of course, with a cast of four or five actors it is considerably easier to show a series of events than it is as a monologuist. But your challenge is nonetheless the same: not to merely speak or tell things, but to do everything you can to *relive* them. This means you should not just talk about your feelings, but try to "paint them" for your audience.

Flesh out scenes with your hands, convey emotions with your voice and thoughts with your eyes. And don't stop there. If a prop is relevant and effective, don't hesitate to use it. To make his monologues as appealing to the eye as possible, Spalding Gray uses maps, lighting changes, music, sound effects, a pointer, and more.

What does it mean to "physicalize"?

People love chopping wood. In this activity one can immediately see results.

—Albert Einstein

Physicalize is merely a theatrical term for making your performance as physical as possible; in other words, using available physical elements during a performance to make the script as immediate and engaging as possible. Theater is about suspension of disbelief. The audience files into the theater knowing full well that the events they are about to see or stories they are about to hear are mostly fiction. Yet still they want to be transported, to be taken in by these artful lies. They want to *believe,* despite their own knowledge to the contrary.

Your job, then, is nothing less than making the stories you tell as vivid, vital, and as real as possible, to "act them out" and ceaselessly make appeals to the senses of sight and sound. (Taste, smell, and touch are far less commonly explored in the theater!) In this quest, many performers will use their bodies and props to physicalize whatever they happen to be talking about in a moment.

Imagine a simple wooden chair. Can you see it? Can you see its flat seat, four sturdy legs, and three-posted back? That simple chair can be a great many things during a performance. A chair, a person, a wall, a dog, a crib, a bush, a car seat, even a prison (with the chair turned around, your legs straddling it, and your hands gripping the posts like bars). By their very featureless and uninteresting nature, simple archetypal props like chairs, lamps, and glasses of water are surprisingly flexible allies in the performer's quest to animate a thought, feeling, or scene. Such allies are particularly valuable to the lone monologuist.

Your body too is a fine tool, capable of producing an astounding range of forms and sounds. For example, near the end of *Borrowed Breath* I share with the audience an experience I once had of plugging my ears with tissue in the hope of muffling the sounds of a noisy motel neighbor, and how due to my plugged ears, I ended up hearing the sound of my own beating heart. To add to the performance of this recollection, as I sit in a chair onstage, I begin to tap my feet, mimicking a heartbeat as I continue to talk. I tap my feet quietly at first, then louder and louder to mirror my own experience of that night in bed lying in the motel. Simple, but effective.

WHY DO SCIENTISTS OFTEN LOOK LIKE GEEKS?

Before I answer this question, allow me to remind you that the word *geek* first gained prominence back in the days of the traveling circus. Alongside the bearded lady and the tiniest man in the world, the sideshow geek was a ragged, half-crazed man who would seem to bite the neck of a live chicken and drink its blood. Not very scientific. Nor did he look much like the now cliché image of the modern scientist—short hair, glasses, a white lab coat, and a breast pocket full of pens, a person who is, almost tragically, more analytical than emotional. A bit of a stiff. A socially awkward wimp. You get the picture. This, then, has become the modern equivalent of the geek. As for the reason why many scientists look this way, frankly I haven't a clue. Maybe after all that chicken blood they like having a lot of pens around so they are always sure to have some colored liquid on hand. And those lab coats *do* look a lot like butchers' jackets.

While onstage, what should I do with my hands?

There is a vitality, a life force, an energy, a quickening that is translated through you into action, and because there is only one of you in all time, this expression is unique.

—Martha Graham

If you watch people in everyday life, many of them use their hands a great deal when talking. Some use them subtly, others with great gusto, but most of us involve hand motions in our daily conversations. So rather than necessarily trying to think up "new" ways of using your hands onstage, the goal is more to be relaxed enough while onstage to use your hands as expressively and uniquely as you probably do every day.

The theater is about exaggeration and about expressing your thoughts and feelings in a manner that people in the back row of the audience are able to comprehend immediately. Thus being relaxed is important. But so is a certain degree of awareness of your motions. Your bodily communication is very much about balance. To be on one hand so familiar with how you want to move and gesture that you can, in a sense, forget about it. But on the other hand, you must be totally focused every moment on what it is you are attempting to accomplish onstage.

Ultimately, your hands should move as silent supporting actors, instinctively embellishing and making all the more vivid much of what you say and do. If, however, you find it difficult to really relax onstage, and your hands seem heavy and lifeless, don't push them to act other than how they feel. Don't fight it or force it. It will come in its own time. For now, focus on the parts of the performance you feel comfortable with and make the very most of those.

WHAT ABOUT DANCING?

I don't know anything whatsoever about dance, but I do suspect that unless you are professionally trained, dancing alone onstage can look remarkably silly. You have been warned.

DR. KAVORKIAN AND FRIENDS

Do I have to have a "big ego" to perform a monologue?

We cannot escape fear. We can only transform it into a companion that accompanies us on our adventures.

—Susan Jeffers

You don't need a big ego, but I suspect it can sometimes really help. Ego is about insecurity, something most humans can relate to. And one of the many things an insecure ego does is convince a person that she or he has nothing to fear and is in fact astonishingly talented. This of course is almost always untrue, especially when one is first starting out. But believing one's own bullshit can sometimes serve as a welcome protection device, and even as a catalyst. Without such self-deceptions, some of us would never dream of getting up onstage, which would be a real loss for us all. However, in the long run it is absolutely essential to get past the insecure preening of fearful ego and establish a confidence based upon authentic experience.

Is it scary to perform a monologue?

The universe will reward you for taking risks on its behalf.

—Shakti Gawain

I certainly thought it was scary when I first started. Back then, I even had a tough time sleeping the night before a performance, a hundred and one worries parading through my mind. Would I remember my lines? Would people find what I said interesting? Would anyone show up? Would they laugh at the funny parts or just sit there, blink, and clear their throats? But fortunately (as with most things) with practice

I became calmer and more assured. That's a big part of the challenge, the fun, and the power of the experience—the potential to grow, not despite not knowing, but *because* of not knowing. Whether or not you believe in a God or a higher power, in times of anxiety you may want to remember the classic serenity prayer: God grant me the serenity to accept the things I cannot change, the courage to change the things I can, and the wisdom to know the difference.

WHAT IS THE BEST THING TO DO WHEN ENCOUNTERING A STREET MIME?

Well, if at all possible, it's of course preferable to avoid them altogether. But if, while walking down the street minding your own business, you suddenly come face to face with some mute, white-faced panhandler, my advice is to look him straight in the eyes, reach deep into your pocket, and then *mime* putting some change into his hat. Sure he'll be pretty miffed, but what's he going to say?

Should I try to be funny?

Concentration is not staring hard at something. It is not trying to concentrate.

—W. Timothy Gallwey

Be funny if you *are* funny. One of the true keys of performance art is to know your strengths, and though I would not advise you to explore only these strengths, I do believe you should make a real effort to showcase them—to share the best of yourself and the truths of your experience that you are most adept at conveying in an engaging fashion.

But what if you don't know your strengths? Well in that case, try everything! Comedy, tragedy, music, drama ... Exploration is essential, especially when you are first learning something. All too soon prejudices form that will severely limit yourself and your shows. But whether you want to explore humor, drama, or whatever, be brave, be honest, and be real.

Beware trying too hard, though. I know, it sounds like some circular New Age mantra, but as someone once said, "People ruin a great many things by trying too hard." Trying too hard can be a real mistake, especially in the theater. The reason why so many brilliant performers "make it look effortless" is because they have worked so long and have for so many years watered their talents with a daily mixture of blood, sweat, and tears that for them ... it *is* effortless. Few things worth having can be rushed, pushed, or cajoled into existence. Don't try too hard. It *will* come, but in its own time.

Is there a difference between performing a monologue during the day and at night?

During the night there tends to be less available natural light. But that aside, the most significant difference between day and night will be in the psychology of the audiences. I've performed monologues during both the afternoon and the evening, and I often have found that afternoon audiences seem less cohesive, consisting more of individuals and couples. Also, people are still at least a little bit in work mode and seem more easily distracted.

In contrast, I find night audiences tend to gel into a single group more readily. They are also usually more focused and invest more emotionally in the performance. Conseqently, they seem more responsive. But remember, all rules, especially in the arts, are at best only broad generalizations. Exceptions are ubiquitous.

What is it like to take a show on the road?

It's quite rare for monologuists, unless you achieve the success of someone like Spalding Gray, Sandra Bernhard, Lily Tomlin, or Eric Bogosian. Yet many monologuists still end up taking their shows to festivals and small venues in other towns and cities. If you are so fortunate, however much

EXTREMELY LACTOSE INTOLERANT

exciting and interesting stuff there may be to see in another town, don't forget what you are there for: to perform. To share your perception and hard work. If you are not accustomed to it, living out of a suitcase can be very draining. Get lots of sleep and if you can, make a point of getting to the local Y or some other gym for a bit of exercise. Regular workouts (even just stretching) will do wonders for your energy on stage as well as your sleep at night.

Another challenge of life on the road is finding decent food. Burgers and pizza are everywhere, but if you don't have a car to drive around, finding fresh fruit and vegetables isn't always easy. I try to grab a bag of baby carrots whenever possible. They keep pretty well, and they act like an antidote for some of the poison you'll undoubtedly eat. As for security in your hotel room, be sure to leave on a light and the television whenever going out. Better safe than depressed.

And remember, if your hotel (more likely a motel!) has an iron, but no ironing board available to guests, just put a towel on the floor. And if they have neither iron nor board, don't fret. Just put your shirt and pants on a hanger in the bathroom (there's usually a hook on the back of the door), turn on the hot shower water, and close the door. Five minutes later your clothes will look as if they were professionally steam cleaned. Seriously. But be sure to do this early in the day; sometimes the clothes get a little damp, and you will need to hang them in the closet to dry off a bit. I admit, I've gone onstage more than a few times in slightly damp clothes. Not much fun.

8

The Television Production

Should I videotape my monologue?

Painting is just another way of keeping a diary.

—Pablo Picasso

Definitely tape your show. Even if you are not planning ever to perform your monologue again, you should nonetheless have a friend or (even better) a professional camera operator tape it. Such a tape is an invaluable source of learning, and if you watch it repeatedly you will learn a great deal not only about how you personally perform, but also about the craft of monologuing in general.

A videotape is also a precious record, documenting a show you probably invested a lot of your thought and time in. Whether for yourself or for others, a videotape is a marvelous thing to be able to watch again years later. It is also an irreplaceable promotional tool, whether you are applying for a performance venue during a festival, trying to interest potential producers, or even trying to promote your show by sending a tape to a local television station in the hope that they will air a few seconds of it during their "what's on around town" segment.

However, a word of warning. When you watch yourself on video, you are not, I repeat, you are *not,* seeing yourself the way other people see you. Don't fall into that trap. No two people see (read "experience") a performance in quite the same way. But there's no doubt about just how eye-opening watching yourself can be—all those little things you weren't aware of, the pauses, the tics, the highly personal symptoms of your possible lack of experience. But do not take these "discoveries" too much to heart. Better simply to note them and move on.

I'm reminded of the centipede who once happened upon an ant. As the centipede approached the ant, the ant asked, "Excuse me, but how is it that you are able to move every one of your hundred legs in perfect harmony?" The cen-

tipede thought for several moments and then said, "Hmmm, that's a good question. I have no idea, and I admit, I have never even questioned it before. Anyway, it's been nice chatting, but I really must get going. Have a nice day." And with that the centipede began to go on his way...and tripped for the first time in his life.

WHEN WAS THE FIRST SNOWMAN MADE?

Just after lunch on February 2, 1852. Susan and Robert Shadworth (the children of John Albert Shadworth and Melissa Dorothy McFadden) had been suspended from school for the day for having kicked a nun in the stomach and burned several churches to the ground. Having nothing better to do, the children went outside to play and decided to mock their principal (Stephen "Two Bruises" Campbell) by making a comical likeness of him out of snow. Well-known for both his considerable girth and stovepipe hat, Campbell was in fact the original inspiration for the now classic snowman. Incidently, after assembling that very first snowman, Susan and Robert tried to set it ablaze, but with little success. Which just goes to show you that, though idle hands may well be the devil's playthings, they also tend to make a lot of cool stuff.

How can I get producers interested in taping my monologue for television?

Promotion is not unlike a stage performance, in that it is first and foremost about getting people's attention. Without that, everything else fails. So the question of promotion and advertising is really about getting, and ideally keeping, the attention of certain key decision makers. However, as with all things, there are ways that will work for you and ways that will work against you.

For instance, let's say that you have written a monologue about obscenity, during which you talk about everything from graffiti to porn movies. Calling a television producer and leaving the most filthy, foul-mouthed message you can possibly imagine will certainly (1) get his attention, (2) be quite memorable, and (3) be relevant to the theme of your monologue. But I suspect there's a much better chance of it working against you than for you. Appealing to people's imaginations is always an excellent idea, especially in promotions, but the goal is to charm or intrigue, not to irk, annoy, and possibly offend.

Several years ago, I wanted to get the attention of a certain television producer, and I realized that he received dozens of proposals and phone calls every day. So I decided to take a bit of a risk, both economically and artistically, and spent seventy-five dollars on a faux leather briefcase, filled it with fifty pounds of loose chocolate M&M's, tossed in one of my blank promotional postcards, and wrapped the briefcase in brown paper. Then on the outside of the package, along with the producer's name and title, in large bold letters I simply wrote the words, BRIBE ENCLOSED. That afternoon, I had it couriered over to the producer's office and nervously waited, wondering if and when I would ever hear back from him.

The *very next day* he left a message on my service, sounding both tickled and impressed, suggesting we set up a time to meet. Several months later, when we taped a show for television, I had everyone from camera operators to wardrobe people actually coming up to me and commenting on the "briefcase filled with M&M's" they had either heard about or personally eaten from. I mention this story not for the sake of my ego, but rather as a humble testament to the power of an imaginative piece of promotion. Truthfully, I am not so much proud about having supposedly "thought it up" as I am grateful to the idea, for having presented itself to me.

WHAT'S UP WITH THOSE BATTERY-OPERATED PEPPER GRINDERS? YOU KNOW, THE ONES WITH THE SMALL, BRIGHT LIGHT ON THE BOTTOM?

I admit, I don't quite understand these things either. What's the light for? In case you get lost in the kitchen? So you can wave it in the air to attract the attention of any search planes? Or maybe it's for those who enjoy eating a caesar salad in a mine shaft. What's next, a salt shaker with a tiny umbrella on it?

How do directors, producers, and camera people adapt monologues for television?

Art does not reproduce the visible; rather, it makes it visible.
—Norma Jean Harris

An entire book could easily be written on this subject alone, and no doubt by a much more qualified and informed writer. But in my experience, when a monologue is adapted for television, it is not uncommon for an even greater emphasis to be put on the visual than was during the theatrical performances. Producers and directors are keenly aware of the limits of the average televison viewer's attention span. In fact, while during the 1960s and 1970s directors routinely spent ten or even fifteen seconds on one shot before cutting to another, today a six- or seven-second shot is now almost standard. Of course, a monologue is very unlike a situation comedy or drama, and given the single performer within a single context, the form doesn't present anywhere near the same number of natural opportunities for cutaways.

Directors, producers, and camera people ask themselves, How can we shoot this monologue so that it is as interesting to *watch* and *listen to* as possible? The resulting visual and aural treatments often add much to the monologue, but in

Advantage, Reaper

adding they also almost always dramatically change its feel, if not the actual narrative. And as you will see by watching even just a few minutes of one of Spalding Gray's or Eric Bogosian's beautifully produced shows, there are a wide range of techniques and devices producers can employ to make a monologue that much more watchable and effective.

But this doesn't make such a production better than a live performance, only *different*. After all, a live performance has a million and one means of connection and involvement that the standard television experience cannot possible duplicate.

HOW MUCH WOOD COULD A WOODCHUCK CHUCK IF A WOODCHUCK COULD CHUCK WOOD?

To answer this perennial question, you must really try to put yourself in the paws of the average woodchuck. Just imagine how it must feel to be a creature commonly referred to by a name that strongly suggests you are capable of executing an activity of which you are, in fact, utterly incapable, i.e. the chucking of wood. How would you feel? Resentful, I suspect. Probably bitter. Perhaps even angry on some unconscious woodchuck level. So if (let's just say) you one day found yourself, a law-abiding peaceful woodchuck, suddenly able to perform the one activity that was your namesake, I believe you would in all likelihood set about chucking an enormous quantity of wood. Finally having an outlet for your pent-up rage, you would probably believe with all your wee woodland heart that you had much to prove and a great deal of catching up to do. Go, woodchuck, go.

Interview with Paul McConvey

In 1996 I was fortunate enough to have *Contents under Pressure* produced for television. It was produced as part of the Spoken Arts series for the Bravo! channel by the Toronto-based production company Sleeping Giant, whose slogan is "Television That Matters." In February 1998 Paul McConvey, one of the company's executive producers, was kind enough to take some time out of his extremely busy schedule for a short interview.

How long have you been involved in the production of monologues for television?

We started the Spoken Arts series in 1994 as a way of creating new drama for Bravo! They didn't have a lot of money for programming, yet as an arts channel they had to address drama on their channel. One of the ways they do this is by buying already existing material. But the other way, which is very brave of them, is to create new drama. So we went to them and we said, "We have a new way of doing drama. One which fulfills your mandate in order to get drama on your channel. Also, as an innovative channel you want something interesting and different that will set you apart from everyone else." So we created the idea of the Spoken

Arts series, which is monologues. It's a way of providing drama, and I mean fictional drama, in a low-budget, very simple production process.

What makes a monologue work on television?

Many of the same qualities that make a regular drama work. When you have an actor and a script that really work together, where the actor has some material that she can sink her teeth into. And when the script is very strong, the drama of that monologue can be just as riveting as any other high-production drama on television.

What percentage of the monologues you have produced are written by the actors who perform them?

The majority of pieces we have done are pieces we found and then brought an actor to. But there are instances, as with your monologue *Contents under Pressure,* where we find an already developed "package," where the material and actor are already developed, and we translate it for television.

What are some of the greatest challenges of this "translation" process?

With a monologue, when an actor is on camera for forty minutes, he is totally naked and vulnerable in a way that, in an assembled piece, he is not. So the first key is finding material that the actor really can *live*. That isn't expository or plot-driven. Monologues can't be plot-driven because there's very little action. But the piece itself has to have an arch, an emotional arch for the actor to get involved in. And therefore, when actors ride that wave, they bring the audience along with them. The most difficult challenge is finding a piece that is emotionally, psychologically, and dramatically engaging for the performer.

How do you film your monologues?

A lot of it is shot close-up, hand-held. The camera gets in the face. It's *right there*. It's six inches, it's eight inches, it's a foot away. That way, it becomes a really intimate portrait of that performer and that text. It also draws the audience in closer. If, that is, they can stand being that close. Some of the audience can't stand being that close to the subject. Even sitting at home watching it on television makes them uncomfortable. But the idea is to bare the performer and to bare the text in such a way that the audience is gripped and sees the entirety and sees right inside it.

What is the difference between a monologue and a speech?

We did a piece called *A Letter to Harvey Milk* [for which Sleeping Giant won a Gemini Award, the Oscars of Canadian television]. The text itself is a short story, and in it an elderly Jewish gentleman tells how he decided to fill up his days by taking a creative writing course. The teacher of the course challenged him to write about something that had meaning for his life. So he used the device of writing letters to a friend, Harvey Milk (the assassinated counselor in San Fransciso). In these letters he told the story of a friend of his in a concentration camp in World War II and about an incident that happened to his friend and, in turn, deeply affected his life. So in the present, this elderly gentleman is telling about something that happened in the past. But he's also *living it at the time*. The emotional reality of that character living in the moment makes it different from a speech. There are lots of monologues where a person or character just gives a concept or presents a set of ideas or a set of instructions or tells about their life in a biographical fashion. But what they don't do in such speeches is live in that moment.

What's the difference between a monologue and a performance of stand-up comedy?

Contents under Pressure was, at first glance, a stand-up comedy piece. But in fact it isn't. There is an inner reality for that character, an inner conflict for that character—a conflict the character either lives out in the course of the monologue or presents for the audience; "This is something I went through, and this is what happened to me." Your monologue was in the moment. I'm a great lover of actors. I think the fact that they get up and do what they do, particularly stand-up comics, is one of the most courageous things in the world. Some do it consciously and some do it unconsciously. I'm not sure that it matters in terms of our appreciation of them. I'm getting a little intellectual here, but I think that as an audience we project a lot of our individuality and our collective needs and desires onto actors and performers. Seeing an actor give a performance where they are right in tune with the material and have an innate understanding of what's being communicated is unbelievably exciting and, for me, gratifying.

The performances of stand-up comics and monologuists both usually have a beginning, a middle, and an end. But a monologuist is not necessarily there strictly to make the audience laugh. She is there to tell a story or to inform the audience of something, whether it is factual or emotional. And remember, viewers ask themselves, Why am I watching this? Why should I invest my energy and time into this monologue or piece? Watching a stand-up comic the answer is, Because I want to laugh. But if it's a monologue, you'd better be giving me more than that. And I'm not implying a monologue is more valuable than stand-up comedy. I'm talking about the performing context.

Is there an ideal length for a monologue?

Well, we usually find that forty minutes is probably about the maximum. On a really strong piece you can maybe stretch it to fifty, fifty-five. That is what we've observed in terms of what we've been doing. A live situation might be different than on camera, especially with the way we shoot them, with a lot of intense close-ups. It's very demanding of the audience. So you can only go so long. Watching them live onstage, I usually find as a viewer my attention starts to lapse after about sixty minutes. I just get tired of the intensity and the need to focus for that length of time.

What are some of the more common mistakes people make when producing monologues for television?

The concept of monologues on television is so simple. There isn't a lot you need to do. You need a good script, a good actor, and a good camera person. That's it. You don't in fact have to do a lot as a producer. The writer, the actor, and the camera are the core elements, and you have to create a setting that allows those three elements to really work together.

What makes for a good camera operator?

Someone who can communicate with the actor *through* the camera. The guy who shot *Contents under Pressure,* Mark McKay, has an innate ability to create a relationship through the camera with the subject. And in fact, Mark in a sense disappears. The actor communicates to the viewer through the camera, so at its best it becomes like a dance between the camera operator and the actor. The camera moves around, not just for the sake of movement but because the movement is somehow "right" in terms of the camera's relationship to the actor at that time. Such an intuitive camera operator is incredibly important and very rare.

What advice can you offer someone writing a monologue?

The pieces that work the best are the ones that have an emotional arc. The character and the audience, through the

script, go on some kind of journey together. There's a beginning, a middle, and a resolution at the end. Now the resolution may be a negative resolution. We might come to
some conclusion about the person that we don't like, and
it's a downer. I don't think that matters. What really matters
is that the actor and the audience have gone on some kind
of emotional journey. The actor's present reality emotionally engaged the audience and took them somewhere.

What advice can you offer someone preparing to perform a monologue?

I guess the only thing I might say is, "At all times you have
to be in that moment." That's where the courage comes in.

A Sitting Meditation

I've been interested in meditation for several years, particularly in regards to relaxing and focusing my energies before a performance. In my readings and discussions with other people I've come across a wide range of meditations for a variety of contexts—staring into campfires, lying down with eyes closed by a running stream, sitting high in a tree in the middle of a still forest, and even meditations involving dead animals, that is, "meditations on the dead" intended to increase one's acceptance of one's own mortality. However, as intriguing and effective as many of these are, very few theater managers allow open fires, tall trees, or dead rabbits in the dressing room.

For use in the theater, one of the most effective meditation exercises I've ever come across I originally found in the back of Jack Kornfield's lovely book *Buddha's Little Instruction Book* (1994). It is not especially different from many other "seated" meditations, but I guess when I read it, something about it struck a chord in me. Do not be fooled by its apparent simplicity. It is not, strictly speaking, "difficult," but as with all forms of meditation, it will take some practice to begin to feel comfortable and reap emotional, psychological, and spiritual benefits. And incidently, if the idea of meditating seems a little too New Age for you, simply think of it as focused relaxation. (I sincerely hope *that* doesn't sound too trendy or arcane for you!)

All right, let's say you are in your dressing room and scheduled to perform in half an hour. You're "in costume," everything you need is onstage (including your glass of water), and you have left instructions with the house manager or one of your assistants to let you know when it's ten minutes to curtain. Everything is prepared . . . stop fretting! Save your energy for the stage! You know your lines, your blocking, your emotional throughlines, so take some time to relax, focus your energies, and "find your center."

Slowly lower yourself into a chair (ideally one with a cushion) and sit in an upright yet relaxed position. Your back should be perfectly straight, but gently, as if you are a king or queen accustomed to sitting in such a pose for hours on end. Slowly close your eyes and then take a few minutes to bring your attention to your immediate thoughts, feelings, and sense of your surroundings. Don't reach for thoughts and impressions. Rather, let them come to you.

Feel the sensations of your body, your physical self. The floor under your feet, your hands in your lap. And also take a moment to notice any sounds around you. Notice all you can, but be sure to let these noticings "go" rather than holding onto any one impression for more than a few moments. Allow yourself to become more still with each passing minute.

Having let your mind survey your surroundings, allow it finally to come to rest on your own breathing. Feel the in-and-out of the breath in your chest as it rises and falls, and in your throat and nose as your breath passes through both. Focus on the rhythm of your breathing and let any other sounds or thoughts come and go like ocean waves in the background.

Sometimes you will find your attention carried away by a memory or physical sensation. And that's fine. What matters is that you do not *hold onto* any of these. Acknowledge them with a simple label such as *remembering* or *itching* or *distraction*, let them pass, and then return your attention to your breathing. You will find that sometimes it will be easy to return your full focus to your breath, and sometimes it will be difficult. No matter. Just go with the flow of it and continue to be aware of your breathing as best you can.

Sit there in that chair, slowly breathing and focused on your breathing, for ten or fifteen minutes. Then slowly open your eyes, but don't get up immediately. Take another few moments to look around at your surroundings and reacquaint yourself with the room. Then get up and calmly, gently, begin to focus your attention on the task at hand. Your performance.

Fringe Festivals

Here is a listing of some fringe festivals from all over the world. It was compiled in January 1999, and though it is far from a complete list, the festival nearest you will be able to give you more information.

United States

Covington Fringe Festival
Louisiana
(504) 735-0707
E-mail: BrookAkya@aol.com

Minnesota Fringe Festival
P.O. Box 580648
Minneapolis, Minnesota 55458-0648
(612) 823-6005

Orlando International Fringe Festival
398 West Amelia Street
Orlando, Florida 32803
(407) 648-0077 Fax: (407) 648-1377
Website: www.orlando.com/fringe

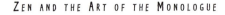

San Francisco Fringe Festival
156 Eddy Street
San Francisco, California 94102
(415) 931-1094 Fax: (415) 931-2699
E-mail: mail@sffringe.org

Seattle Fringe Festival
7400 Sand Point Way NE, Building 30
Seattle, Washington 98115
(206) 526-1959 Fax: (206) 526-1988
E-mail: fringe@wolfenet.com

Canada

Calgary Fringe Festival
1229 Ninth Avenue S.E.
Calgary, Alberta T2G 0S9
(403) 269-1444
E-mail: fringe@loosemoose.com

Edmonton Fringe Festival
#300, 10330 Eighty-fourth Avenue
Edmonton, Alberta T6E 2G9
(403) 448-9000 Fax: (403) 431-1893
E-mail: fta@alberta.com

Montreal Fringe Festival
C.P.42013 succursale Jeanne-Mance
Montreal, PQ, H2W 2T3
(514) 849-3378 Fax: (514) 849-5529
E-mail: www.montrealfringe.ca

Ottawa Fringe Festival
#240-2 Daly Avenue
Ottawa, Ontario K1N 6E2
(613) 232-6162 Fax: (613) 569-7660
E-mail: fringe@storm.ca

Toronto Fringe Festival
720 Bathurst Street, Suite 303
Toronto, Ontario M5S 2R4
(416) 534-5919 Fax: (416) 534-6021
E-mail: fringe@fringetoronto.com

Vancouver Fringe Festival
1163 Commercial Drive
Vancouver, British Columbia V5L 3X3
(604) 257-0350 Fax: (604) 253-1924
E-mail: thefringe@ultranet.ca

Victoria Fringe Festival
3rd Floor, 1205 Broad Street
Victoria, British Columbia, V8W 2A4
(205) 383-2663 Fax: (250) 380-1999
E-mail: intrepid@bc.sympatico.ca

Winnipeg Fringe Festival
174 Market Avenue
Winnipeg, Manitoba R3B 0P8
(204) 956-1340 Fax: (204) 947-3741
E-mail: fringe@mtc.ca

Scotland

Edinburgh Fringe Festival
Phone: 131 226 5257
Fax: 131 220 4205
E-mail: admin@edfringe.com

Australia

Adelaide Fringe Festival
Phone: 618 8231 7760
Fax: 618 8231 5080
E-mail: buzz@adelaidefringe.com.au

Hong Kong

Hong Kong Fringe Festival
Phone: 852 2521 7251
Fax: 852 2868 4415

Selected Bibliography and Videography

Books

Capra, Fritjof. *The Tao of Physics.* New York: Bantam, 1977.

Cleary, J. C. *Zen Dawn.* Boston: Shambala, 1986.

Gray, Spalding. *Impossible Vacation.* New York: Vintage Books, 1993.

Hanh, Thich Nhat. *Zen Keys.* New York: Anchor Press, 1974.

Herrigel, Eugen. *Zen in the Art of Archery.* New York: Vintage Books, 1953.

Kapleau, Philip. *The Three Pillars of Zen.* Garden City, NY: Doubleday, 1980.

Kornfield, Jack. *Buddha's Little Instruction Book.* Toronto: Bantam, 1994.

Lao-tzu. *Tao Te Ching.* Translated by D. C. Lau. New York: Penguin, 1963.

Mamet, David. *True and False: Heresy and Common Sense for the Actor.* New York: Pantheon Books, 1997.

Meisner, Sanford. *Sanford Meisner on Acting.* New York: Vintage Books, 1987.

Sankey, Jay. *Zen and the Art of Stand-up Comedy.* New York: Routledge, 1998.

Senzaki, Nyogen, and Ruth McCandless. *Buddhism and Zen.* San Francisco: North Point Press, 1987.

Winokur, Jon. *Zen to Go.* New York: Plume, 1990.

Wood, Ernest. *Zen Dictionary.* Rutland, VT: Tuttle, 1972.

Video

Bernhard, Sandra. *Without You I'm Nothing.* 1990.
Bogosian, Eric. *Confessions of a Porn Star.* 1995.
———. *Funhouse.* 1986.
———. *Sex, Drugs, Rock and Roll.* 1991.
———. *Talk Radio.* 1988.
Gray, Spalding. *Gray's Anatomy.* 1997.
———. *Swimming to Cambodia.* 1987.
———. *Terrors of Pleasure.* 1990.
Miller, Dennis. *Black and White.* 1990.
Murphy, Eddie. *Delirious.* 1983.
Tomlin, Lily. *Search for Signs of Intelligent Life.* 1985.